In a CLASS of its OWN

*Inside the UK's
top school for
the culinary stars
of tomorrow*

By Gary Hunter with Adam Kay

Written by:
Gary Hunter with Adam Kay

Edited by:
Martin Edwards, Christopher Brierley

Design by:
Richard Abbey

Photography by:
© Jodi Hinds Photography
www.jodihinds.com
Additional photographs supplied by Westminster Kingsway College
Pictures of Jamie Oliver supplied by David Loftus

First published in 2013 on behalf of:
Westminster Kingsway College – www.westking.ac.uk

Published by:
RMC Books – www.rmcbooks.co.uk

Contents

In A Class of Its Own: Inside The UK's Top
School for The Culinary Stars of Tomorrow

Welcome to...
'The Hogwarts of Culinary Schools'.

We have often been compared to this mythical school in recent times and it may be slightly tongue in cheek and mentioned in jest, but there does appear to be some similarity if you look close enough.

Our Culinary Science Laboratory certainly produces many potions, charms and apparitions in the guise of scientific culinary delights that eventually make their way onto our grand plates in the esteemed Escoffier Restaurant. This specialised alchemy is produced by our final year students on the Professional Chef Diploma.

Being a school of magic, many fields of study at Hogwarts differ from the studies of a typical school, and this is the same for our Professional Chef students at Westminster Kingsway College who study the culinary arts and

hospitality subjects of garde manger, butchery, patisserie, bakery, classical cuisine, confectionery, barista, food and beverage service, chocolate, cocktails and spirits, viticulture and oenology, gastronomy, contemporary cuisine, menu engineering and business management. These are compulsory subjects for the first two years and students are able to study their own chosen specialist area in the third year.

Our teaching team are some of the most dedicated, professional, engaging and expert people assembled to drive the students through a curriculum designed to stimulate thought, instil discipline and challenge technical abilities. Admission to our courses is selective, in that students who pass our rigorous and informative interview sessions will be

offered a place onto a course to launch their career in hospitality or culinary arts. Our success rates for students continue to be the highest.

Since its founding in 1910, Westminster Kingsway College has offered leading hospitality and culinary programmes distinguished by its quality, innovation and committed teaching team. Lessons emphasise applied learning in small class settings, and innovations have included the formation of our incredibly successful international competition team and Gastronomic Society. The opportunity for students to learn in our two critically acclaimed restaurants, and undertake wine studies with the addition of management and entrepreneurship, assures that our students build their knowledge and skills in the ideal learning sequence.

The college dynamically carries forward its legacies of education, training, innovation and industry collaboration in its programmes and research through the global impact of our alumni. With the support of the hospitality industry, we continue to lead the way, inspiring excellence the world over. We are confident that the future has never looked better for our graduates and we are proud to share with you the thoughts, secrets, recipes and ideals which are the foundation of this incredible school and encourage you to visit our restaurants or indeed apply to start your journey in the best way possible for a career in this wonderful industry.

Gary Hunter
Head of Culinary Arts & Hospitality

New recruits and a skilled workforce

For over a century Westminster Kingsway College and its predecessor institutes, technical and FE colleges have provided the London hospitality industry with new recruits and a skilled workforce who have shaped the most exciting restaurant and hotel scene in the world. We are proud that our graduates can be found in the best hotel and restaurant kitchens across the world. We often meet Westminster Kingsway College alumni working as chefs, front-of-house or management across all sectors of the hospitality industry. This book is a celebration of the past, present and future of the excellence in training provided by Westminster Kingsway College's School of Hospitality & Culinary Arts. As one of only six Principals during the 100-plus years it covers, I am proud to be associated with it.

Westminster Kingsway College recruits over 15,000 students every year across a range of sectors reflecting the London labour market. The college is so much more than just the School of Hospitality & Culinary Arts but that work lies at our heart and exemplifies everything a 21st century college is about. Government policy on skills rightly promotes the centrality of employer needs in designing and delivering training provision. However, that policy also too often neglects colleges' long experience of working in partnership with business to define requirements and blend expertise in what works most effectively educationally. We believe the relationship Westminster Kingsway College has established with London's hospitality employers exemplifies what can be achieved when a college works side-by-side with the sector it supports in a mutually respectful partnership.

Our continuing reputation amongst potential students and employers is founded on the excellence of the graduates who leave us. In turn, their success is based on the teaching and other experiences they gain whilst training with us. We employ the very best staff who are 'from' and remain 'of' the industry. They are recruited to Westminster Kingsway College directly from the industry on the basis of their passion for their subject, industrial expertise and ability to impart both to those who wish to learn from them. We support them in maintaining their connections with their colleagues in industry through active membership of professional organisations and participation in competitions and other industry activities.

Our staff and students provide pop-up restaurants at trade shows and events so the industry can directly sample what we are about. They enter, and are successful in, competitions with other colleges but also with those professionals still working in the industry. We have recently opened our 15th training kitchen in our base in Vincent Square, Victoria and will be adding more as we embark on the extensive building programme planned for 2014-15. We have three commercial restaurants in Victoria, a café at our Regent's Park Centre and service meetings and conference facilities inside the college and at external venues. The customers eating in our restaurants come from all backgrounds and include gastronauts, those who live or work locally and those who know about our reputation for well prepared, excellent food, served without fuss at a reasonable price. The many regular customers and excellent restaurant reviews published in the national and regional press are testament to the success of this model.

Whatever your previous engagement with Westminster Kingsway College, I hope that in browsing or reading this book you will understand more of our great history and visualise our future in continuing to provide London's hospitality employers with the workforce they need to create a world-beating offer and our students with the opportunity to fulfil their passions and dreams.

Andy Wilson
Principal

Key areas of employment

The School of Hospitality has a long standing reputation for its culinary arts – patisserie, bakery, restaurant food and beverage service and hospitality management education – with a clear focus on delivering the very best training experience for students at all levels embarking on a career in the hospitality sector.

In the 21st century, the hospitality industry has emerged as one of the key areas of employment, offering a wide-ranging and versatile environment in which to carve out worthy and interesting careers. The UK economy appreciates the contribution the hospitality sector makes to both the reputation and wealth of the country. As heavy engineering and manufacturing has diminished in recent times, an energetic food and hospitality service industry has grown up to replace it. Year after year, as the modern employment landscape changes, the hospitality sector expands to accommodate increasing numbers of young people into its ranks. Furthermore, the expectations of a discerning consumer population continue to rise. This places increasingly more exacting demands on the quality of trained graduates.

The UK exists in a highly competitive global tourism market and our hospitality sector has become one of the most important aspects in helping to establish Britain's reputation as an attractive destination. Nowadays, the sector is more of a profession than a trade. It exists as a shop window helping define what Britain has to offer to millions of visitors from overseas. Once more, the quality of our graduates will help contribute to Britain's image, credibility, the strength of its welcome and its ability to entertain and delight visitors to these shores.

Westminster Kingsway College has always sought to ensure that its graduates leave the School with a comprehensive range of skills and knowledge to be able to make an impact in industry and compete for the exciting jobs available. Great emphasis has been placed upon creating strong links with industry partners, from all sectors of hospitality and tourism environments. At all times throughout our long history, the college has sought to bring together a well qualified and experienced teaching team with a clear understanding of the needs of the workplace. The team comprises a range of nationalities reflecting the cosmopolitan nature of this exciting sector. It has responded to the dynamic nature of hospitality and designed its training programmes to reflect the needs of this landscape.

In recent times there has been an even greater focus on partnerships. Employers are central to all that we do within the school. Training content is co-designed with key associates from industry, assessed in partnership with them and enriched and inspired by them. Our colleagues from the world of work receive students on visits, work placements, employ them on trials, offer part-time jobs and present to our students the range of interesting opportunities which exist in their companies. They speak directly with our students through presentations, demonstrations and mentoring support, helping to define what it takes to win the dream job, ahead of progressing onto a variety of career pathways. This book shines the light on the first stages of that journey, giving an insight into each of the key players, the partners and the supporters. It illustrates the trials and tribulations and the challenges of making the grade. It is no longer sufficient to be competent; ordinary is no longer an

option. Today, it is all about attaining the finest achievements and delivering a consistently high standard of skills and knowledge in a highly competitive employment environment.

The better the calibre of our graduates today, the more secure future generations of our graduates will be. Collectively, it is their individual reputations that will combine to represent the strength and credibility of the School of Hospitality and Culinary Arts.

It is a privilege to be the director of this school, and to have witnessed its development, its evolution and the revolution that has occurred during its long history. Enjoy the pages that lie in store for you here.

On reading this book, you will become aware of the complex nature of a highly committed team within the college; their drive to create a balance between challenging, developing and supporting those who choose to study here. You will get a sense of the constant aim to enhance and improve all that is offered to those who attend the programmes. You will get an insight into an establishment dedicated to building the capabilities of all who venture into this exciting institution.

As the stature and influence of the hospitality sector continues to grow, so does the response of this fine college and its expectations of the graduates who pass through its doors. They will get to follow in the footsteps of their predecessors, knowing they have a vital responsibility and

an important role to play. We expect them to continue to learn, to be curious about the world around them, to stride out with confidence and to reach for the opportunities that present themselves. We expect them to make their mark, to be known for their capabilities, personalities, their patience and their excellence. We expect them to be clear in their continued quest for knowledge and skills; to contribute to the collective success of hospitality UK and to remember that they will always remain part of this great institution.

The college continues to surprise and delight generations of learners, visitors, parents, friends and associates as it seeks to grow the fraternity that have become part of it over the years. At each stage of our development, we will continue to improve the status of this sector by ensuring the calibre of successive graduates bring with them even greater levels of skills, knowledge, commitment, excitement and energy to the employers that invest in their futures.

Nowhere is it more clearly in focus than the changing nature of food and service. So, take a moment to look at all that is presented here in these pages – an honest account of the modern vocational training school with all of its constituent parts and personalities. It is a college which has stood the test of time and continues to respond and renew its offer to meet the needs of the rapidly changing world of opportunity.

Geoff Booth
Director of the School of Hospitality

A tremendous start

I am honoured to have been asked to write this foreword. As a former student, member of staff and more recently President of the Old Students' Association, it is with very considerable pride that I can truly say that Westminster Kingsway College has been at the centre of my life and career over some 63 years. I have never met a current or former student who has not demonstrated that same pride or expressed gratitude for the tremendous start that the College gave them.

On the 7th March 1910, Mr R. Blair, Education Officer with the London County Council, wrote to Herman Senn of the Universal Cookery and Food Association as follows: "I am directed to inform you that the council has under consideration of the communication from the Universal Cookery and Food Association urging the establishment of a School of Professional Cookery... agreed to establish in September 1910, a Cookery Technical School (for boys) at the LCC Westminster Technical Institute, Vincent Square...

"The council is anxious to open the school in September and it is important that early steps should be taken to arrange for the appointment of the teachers and the purchase of the equipment."

Could anyone involved at the time ever have believed that their fledgling institution was to become a forerunner of hospitality education and training throughout the world and its brand leader for over 100 years? In fact, many of its former students were influential in the development of hospitality education over those years as members of staff or heads of department in some of the three hundred-plus catering colleges that exist today. Links with Her Majesty's Armed Forces have always been strong, with many former students rising to very senior ranks within each of the services.

The College is justifiably proud of its star successes, people such as Ronald Kinton, co-author of the best selling text book 'Practical Cookery', and Ronald Aubrey, chef of the royal household, along with Jamie Oliver and many more. Westminster Kingsway College's lasting legacy, however, will be the thousands and thousands of former students who have been the very backbone of the hospitality industry, constantly achieving the high standards they were set at the outset of their careers.

This book celebrates a very special place indeed.

Bev Puxley
President of the Old Students' Association

'These people aren't just graduates... they're the culinary stars of tomorrow.'

Proud parents snap photographs with tear-stained fingers. Their subjects shuffle awkwardly, hoods hanging off shoulders, too-big robes billowing. The low rumble of excited, impatient chatter lingers in the air like a dense fog, and the room smells of coffee, poured to pass the time but never drunk. The students spot their former lecturers and greet them like old friends. After all, that's what they are to them now.

In many respects, this graduation day is the same as that of any other educational establishment around the world, that

familiar atmosphere of joy and nervousness, the assembled throng of family and friends and teachers and guests. But it's different in one way.

These students aren't celebrating their achievements in English, or law, or politics. They studied the culinary arts; cooking, patisserie, waiting on tables, restaurant management and everything in between. And they studied these subjects at one of the oldest and best schools of hospitality and culinary arts in the world. These young people aren't just graduates... they're the culinary stars of tomorrow.

Established in 1910, Westminster Kingsway College's school of hospitality and culinary arts has been training budding young chefs and waiters for over a century. As the oldest and most well-known establishment of its type in the UK, its name is synonymous with excellence.

The school was founded by a group of prominent figures in the hospitality industry, including the famous chef Auguste Escoffier, after whom one of its two restaurants is named. Over the years, it has helped to launch the careers of some of the biggest names in the business, including Ronald Kinton, Jamie Oliver, Ainsley Harriott and many, many more.

Today, Westminster Kingsway College remains at the forefront of training in the culinary arts. Its team of staff includes respected professionals from every corner of the industry, people whose personal achievements are matched only by their passion for passing on their skills and knowledge to the next generation. The college continues to move forward, too. Recent refurbishments have seen the introduction of first-rate new kitchen facilities, as well as a state-of-the-art culinary science laboratory, thought to be the first of its kind in the world of further education.

This book celebrates Westminster Kingsway College's enduring legacy. With contributions from esteemed alumni and current staff, it looks at the college's illustrious history and its continuing commitment to its students, from induction to graduation and beyond. It's the definitive document of the place where the culinary stars of tomorrow are born. A place that is, truly, in a class of its own.

History

On both the small and silver screens, there's a common representation of Victorian London as a place of abject poverty and squalor, populated by soot-covered urchins sent to work the second they could walk.

There's truth in this, of course, but it's only one side of the story. The end of the 19th century was also a time of prosperity for the capital. This growth gave rise to the hospitality industry which the City remains famous for

today. And it was this which in turn led to the creation of another London institution, one whose renown continues to grow more than 100 years on: Westminster Kingsway College.

In the late 1880s, a group of prominent figures from the hospitality industry had joined together to form The Culinary Society, later known as the Universal Cookery and Food Association (UCFA) and still in existence today as the

Craft Guild of Chefs (CGOC). The group included Auguste Escoffier, the celebrated French chef widely regarded as the father of modern cooking, and Cesar Ritz, the Swiss hotelier whose grand establishments led to the coining of the term 'ritzy'. Other members included Isidore Salmon, then a chef at his family's firm J. Lyons & Co, Iwan Kriens, a Dutchman serving as chef at the Howard Hotel, and Swiss-born Charles Herman Senn, who was working at the Reform Club.

These men, titans of London's ever-growing hospitality industry, were concerned about the lack of young people available to work in their establishments. While cooking was being taught in schools at this time, it was invariably only to girls. The UCFA's members were also worried about the content and quality of what was being taught; there wasn't much in the way of established guidelines or syllabuses for teachers to work from.

LAROUSSE GASTRONOMIQUE

Emile Lefebvre with a kitchen class in 1957

A view of the restaurant in 1922. Mr Stark is supervising

Not all elements of the courses were practical

THE MODERN BAKER CONFECTIONER & CATERER

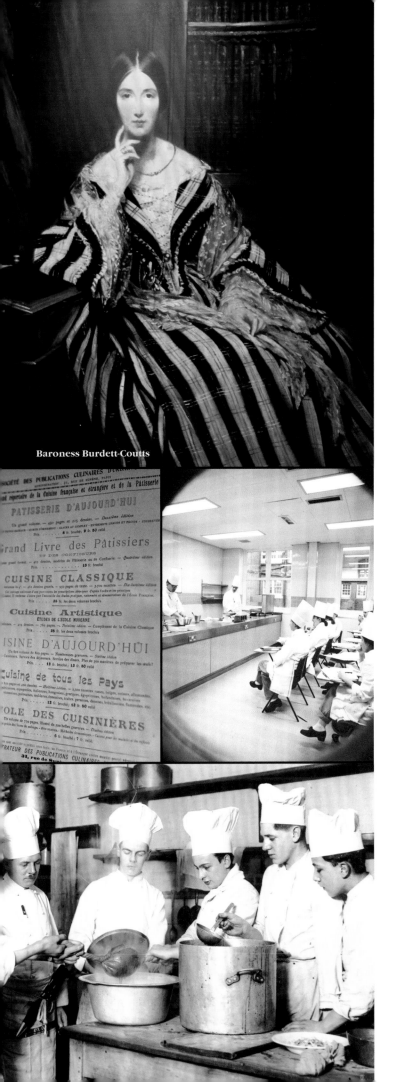

Baroness Burdett-Coutts

Fortunately the Association shared this concern with one of the wealthiest philanthropists of the era. Baroness Burdett-Coutts invested a large portion of her £3million fortune, inherited from her banker grandfather Thomas Coutts, in helping to improve the lives of London's poor. In particular she helped to transform the area around Vincent Square in Westminster, which at that time was impoverished, by founding several schools nearby, as well as St Stephen's Church on Rochester Row.

Burdett-Coutts was especially interested in catering education, and this interest brought her in to contact with the UCFA. She and her husband William became patrons of the Association (William also became one of its presidents), and it was partly thanks to the couple's influence that, in the early 1900s, the UCFA could begin holding cookery classes for boys.

Initially, these classes were held at various different schools in the Westminster area, as well as the National Training School of Cookery, an institution offering domestic cooking lessons for girls in South Kensington. Before long, however, the Association was able to open its own cookery school, on Vauxhall Bridge Road, teaching the type of cooking skills required by chefs in high-end hotels and establishments.

Demand for places quickly increased, and the running of the school placed a strain on the Association's limited financial resources. As a result, the group began negotiations with the London County Council (LCC) about a new school of cookery, to be opened by the council.

A consultative committee was set up to hold these negotiations. The committee included Auguste Escoffier and Iwan Kriens, and was chaired by Isidore Salmon, who was by now an LCC councillor, with Charles Herman Senn serving as vice-chairman. The UCFA members sitting on the committee were able to offer their expert advice to the council about what exactly would be required in terms of equipment, facilities and formulating a curriculum. The venue eventually chosen for the new school was the Westminster Technical Institute in Vincent Square, a training establishment set up a few years earlier by Baroness Burdett-Coutts.

On the 27th of September 1910, the LCC School of Cookery at the Westminster Technical Institute, the first dedicated catering college in the country, was born. Iwan Kriens, previously superintendent of the school at Vauxhall Bridge Road, was installed as headmaster, a position he would hold for the next 25 years.

The first set of students studied a course called the Cookery Technical Day School, which covered every aspect of professional cooking. A century on, there have, of course, been changes – the course is now called the Professional Chef Diploma, and it's taught at what's now known as Westminster Kingsway College. But the school's principle aim – to provide aspiring young chefs with an outstanding education – remains firmly in place today.

Over the past 100-plus years, Westminster Kingsway College has grown bigger and better than its founders could ever have anticipated. The college has undergone continual changes and improvements that have pushed it towards the respected position it enjoys today. And those improvements started pretty much from the word go.

A couple of years after the school opened, it became clear that an outlet for the food being produced was needed. As a result, a training restaurant was opened, serving food prepared by students to the public. This is what's now known as The Vincent Room Brasserie.

At the same time, staff recognised the need for trained waiting staff who could serve in the restaurant. A new two-year Restaurant Trainees Course was therefore developed, in which students were taught the basic principles of waiting on customers, reception duties and general restaurant management. The first waiting instructor was Albert Stark.

With the onset of World War I in 1914, many students and staff who were of age were called into duty. Iwan Kriens – by all accounts a formidable and charismatic man – carried on teaching the remaining students single-handedly, supported by teachers from the Board of Education and the Ministry of Food. Classes of cooks and manageresses from the Army and Air Force canteens, as well as men from the Royal Army Medical Corps, came to Westminster Kingsway College, learning in particular about food economy. This period inspired Kriens to write his 'Victory Cookery Book,' featuring ration-friendly recipes and instructions on how to cook without fat or flour.

It took a while for classes to get going again after the war but by 1922 they were in full swing again with the re-opening of the Brasserie, now with the addition of a licensed bar. In the post-war recession of the late 1920s and early 1930s, more new courses were added, including short courses for ex-servicemen and unemployed miners.

In 1932, the institute underwent a series of major extensions, including the addition of a larder and pastry areas and the installation of large-scale catering equipment. The year 1934 sadly saw the death of Charles Herman Senn, the enthusiastic man who, as secretary of the UCFA and vice-chairman of the consultative committee, had played a huge role in the founding of the school. That same year, Iwan Kriens set up the Old Pupils' Association, for the purpose of, amongst other things, organising social events for alumni. The group was renamed the Old Students' Association in 1948 and remains active to this day. In 1936, 'Papa' Kriens, as he was affectionately known, retired from his position as headmaster.

In 1939, construction began on a 50-room training hotel, but due to the outbreak of World War II it was never completed. The Vincent Square building was requisitioned and the school was moved to semi-permanent premises in Clapham. From here, the students were evacuated, some to Exeter, some to Brighton, until around a year later when teaching was moved to Beare Green in Surrey.

Apart from being struck by an incendiary bomb, which burned a top floor room, the Vincent Square building survived the war undamaged, and teaching soon returned. In 1947, girls were admitted onto the chef's course for the first time, while in 1949 the institute became Westminster Technical College, and restricted its admissions to school leavers aged 16 and over.

In the early 1950s, the restaurant received another large-scale extension, including further kitchens and a new wine cellar. These extensions culminated in the opening of another restaurant, the Escoffier Room, named after the school's famous founding father. The official opening ceremony took place in November 1953 and was attended by the mayor of Westminster, the college governing body, the French ambassador and relatives of the late Sir Isidore Salmon, who had been knighted in 1933 for "political and public services". Plaques honouring Salmon and Escoffier were unveiled; the plaque to Escoffier was presented by the Association Culinaire Française, another culinary organisation which the great man founded.

In 1977, the college received a donation of approximately 2,000 items formerly belonging to the photographer Lee Miller from her husband Sir Roland Penrose. Miller, along with Penrose and her former lover Man Ray, was a noted collector of art and photography, but she was also a culinary enthusiast. The items donated to the college after her death

The gentleman stood up on the right is Auguste Escoffier. Three along from him is Iwan Kriens

Westminster Technical Institute

Principal - J. N. LONG, D.Sc. (London) M.I.Mech.E.

◐

THE

Magazine

of the

Hotel and Restaurant

Junior Technical School

1937-1938

Headmaster - A. C. MARSHALL, B.Com. (Lond.), F.R.Econ.S.

Head of Cookery Department - JOHN VINCENT

Head Waiter Instructor - N. L. W. BARRETT

1974 Restaurant Operations Course

LA CUISINE CLASSIQUE
ÉTUDES PRATIQUES, RAISONNÉES ET DÉMONSTRATIVES
DE L'ÉCOLE FRANÇAISE
par
URBAIN DUBOIS & ÉMILE BERNARD
ANCIENS CHEFS DE CUISINE DE LL. MM., L'EMPEREUR ET L'IMPÉRATRICE D'ALLEMAGNE

Below: A view of the restaurant in the early 1930s

included cookery books and other culinary artefacts which formed the basis for what would become the Westminster Gastronomy Collection. Along with later donations from the Association Culinaire Française, including several books relating to Escoffier, and legendary chef Michel Bourdin, as well as material from the college's own archives, today it represents one of the finest collections of culinary arts and gastronomy texts in the country.

In March 1985, the college's kitchens were closed for a £2.2 million refurbishment. This meant that The Vincent Rooms restaurants had to close, and 150 students had to be found work in industry. The redesigned facilities were ready in time for the start of the next academic year, and included three new production kitchens, as well as further improvements to the restaurants.

The college entered the new millennium with another name change, thanks to a merger in 2000 with London's Kingsway College. The college's culinary arts department was also named a Centre of Vocational Excellence (CoVE) by the Learning and Skills Council, in recognition of the high standards of teaching on offer and the department's strong links with industry.

In 2006, the now-Westminster Kingsway College received more new cooking facilities with the opening of the Electrolux Escoffier Kitchen. As its name suggests, the kitchen contains state-of-the-art Electrolux equipment and is used to service the Escoffier Room restaurant.

2010 was a truly landmark year for Westminster Kingsway College, as it marked a century of culinary education at the college. Centenary celebrations were held throughout the year, beginning with a visit from His Royal Highness the Prince of Wales. Events included a centenary end-of-year ball for hospitality students, an exhibition of the college's photographic and archive material, an afternoon tea for the Old Students' Association and Christmas lunches held in The Vincent Rooms, with menus which featured dishes from throughout the school's unique 100-year history.

The centenary offered an opportunity to reflect, but the Westminster Kingsway College School of Culinary Arts and Hospitality – as it is known today – continues to look to the future as well. In 2012, two more cutting-edge kitchens and a science facility were installed at the college – the Baroness Burdett-Coutts Kitchen; the Chocolate Laboratory, an upgrade of the Cacao Barry Patisserie; and the Culinary Science and Kitchen Innovation Laboratory. The 12-stationed Baroness Burdett-Coutts Kitchen, supported by Vitamix and Churchill, is named after the college's famous benefactor and features the latest cookery ranges, multimedia facilities and a separate demonstration area.

Perhaps even more exciting are the other two kitchens, both thought to be the only facilities of their kind in any further education college in the UK. The Chocolate Laboratory and The Cacao Barry Patisserie, sponsored by Cacao Barry and Barry Callebaut, feature specialist equipment that conches the cocoa bean, allowing students to learn about the process involved in creating chocolate as well as its use in a variety of recipes. The Culinary Science and Kitchen Innovation Laboratory, meanwhile, is dedicated to the training of and research into culinary science and gastronomy. Helmed by renowned food scientist and Westminster Kingsway College lecturer Dr Rachel Edwards-Stuart, the laboratory is used to teach kitchen science to Professional Chef Diploma students, as well as courses and seminars for chefs and caterers and research into culinary science and gastronomic sciences. The laboratory contains equipment from sponsors such as Cream Supplies, Labogene, Kitchen Aid, Control Induction and EOwater, including a rotary evaporator, an ultrasonic homogeniser, a centrifuge, an anti-griddle, water baths, a sous-vide oven, a chamber vacuum machine and a dehydrator.

Hi-tech equipment, futuristic cooking techniques... clearly, a lot has changed over the past century at the former LCC School of Cookery at the Westminster Technical Institute. These changes and improvements continue. For much of 2013, the Vincent Square building has been encased in scaffolding as renovation work is carried out to the building's exterior, including that of The Vincent Rooms restaurants. Through all the years of change, one goal has remained constant: that the culinary arts and hospitality education on offer here at Westminster Kingsway College is the finest in the world. The vision that Escoffier, Salmon et al had for this place has been fulfilled a thousand times over, and it's their esteemed legacy which continues to inspire the college's students and staff to this day.

Students

Y ou don't decide on a career in the hospitality industry if you want an easy ride. This line of work is notoriously one of the most difficult, marked by long, unsociable hours and high levels of stress. There can be great rewards for the best chefs and waiters, of course, but cushy jobs they most certainly are not.

There are great rewards for Westminster Kingsway College's culinary arts and hospitality students, too, not least

the first-rate qualifications they end up with after they've completed their chosen course. But that doesn't mean these youngsters are wrapped up in cotton wool – on the contrary, the college aims to provide them with a realistic insight into what life in the industry is like, which means hard work and plenty of it. It's an ethos the students are introduced to before they've even enrolled.

"We'll prepare some fermenting bread dough and do a

quick demonstration of manipulation into different bread roll shapes, and see whether they can recreate that demonstration," says Gary Hunter, head of hospitality and culinary arts.

He's talking about the initial interview process that all candidates face, which involves them completing a series of different tasks. "We look at their dexterity, we look at their ability to be able to take on board simple instructions, and

see whether they can complete that in a certain amount of time, to our standards."

Those exacting standards are the same as those of any top-flight restaurant or hotel, as potential Westminster Kingsway College students discover almost immediately. For most, their first introduction to the college is an open day; there are usually around four held throughout the year. Once they've attended one of these, candidates are encouraged to submit their applications as early as possible. And with good reason: in June 2013, the college was taking applications for the 2014-15 academic year.

Successful applicants are invited to interview sessions, which take place on Saturdays from December through to June. These are no stuffy, formal chats, but full-day sessions with busy and varied itineraries. As well as the bread roll task, candidates take part in various other exercises. These include a food recognition test, in which they're asked to identify assorted fruit, vegetables and herbs which have been laid out across large kitchen tables, and a taste test, which sees them tasting flavoured jellies which are deliberately coloured in a confusing way – the red ones don't taste of strawberry or raspberry as one would expect, for example. Short cookery skill tests, written culinary tests, coffee meetings with parents and guardians and personal one-to-one interviews are also undertaken.

Candidates also have lunch at the interview sessions, which is served to them by current Westminster Kingsway College students. Gary and his team receive feedback about the candidates from the students, finding out whether they are asking questions and showing enthusiasm at this early stage.

"It's about us looking to see how they socially interact with each other," says Gary.

The interview sessions aren't just for the candidates, however, as Gary explains. "We encourage and expect our candidates to bring their parents, carers or guardians along with them, because we want them to understand that coming to Westminster Kingsway College is a big step in

their education process and the first step into their career, he says. "They also need to understand – because we get a lot of applications from outside London – quite what it's like to travel into the City on a daily basis and the support that we can offer."

In total, around 500 candidates will be invited to the interview sessions. They are competing for, on average, between 160 and 170 places on the Professional Chef Diploma first year course alone, and there are other culinary arts and hospitality courses within the department too. With competition being so fierce, there will inevitably be disappointments – even talented candidates may miss out. But, as Gary explains, that's a reflection of those exacting Westminster Kingsway College standards. Just being talented isn't enough.

"I want our students to come here with great ambitions," says Gary. "I don't want them to come here to learn at Westminster Kingsway College and then go back to their village or town to be a chef at their local pub, because they might as well go to their local college to do that. We're looking for students that want to make a difference in the industry."

The lucky ones will be the people who Gary and his team feel will make that difference – the ones who show real potential from the outset, and will almost certainly go on to become the culinary stars of tomorrow. Once those chosen few have received and accepted their offer of a place here at Westminster Kingsway College, the hard work can really begin.

Of all the courses offered by Westminster Kingsway College's School of Hospitality and Culinary Arts, the most historical is the Professional Chef Diploma. This full-time, three-year course is the spiritual successor of the Cookery Technical Day School, the programme delivered by Messrs Salmon, Senn and Kriens when the college first opened in 1910.

The course has moved on a fair bit since then, obviously, but its aim remains the same: to deliver a rounded programme of learning that covers every single aspect of the hospitality trade. For the new intake of students, that extensive curriculum means the hard work starts from day one.

"It's a really, really full programme of learning, opportunities and experiences in the first year," says Gary Hunter. "They will learn the basics of cookery, food and beverage service, patisserie and garde manger."

Paul Jervis, course co-ordinator for the first year programme, believes that the Professional Chef Diploma offers students a truly comprehensive learning experience. "What we've got now is a really good balance," he says. "They're learning the fundamentals – baking, roasting, boiling, steaming, poaching – but they're also learning modern trends, current techniques."

From the outset, students are taught to excel and to go over and above what's expected of them. "Our first years will have already learned some of the skills towards different preparation methods for fish, and butchery, which is actually a Level 2 skill," says Paul, himself an ex-Westminster Kingsway College student. "Once you've got that foundation in place in the first year, you can then expand on it much more quickly in the second year."

As with any great college, the first year here is also geared towards building up student confidence and helping them make the transition from young men and women to adults, as Paul explains. "Some of them will come to college quite shy at 16 years of age, but in the second year, they're far more able to deal with talking to adults in a working environment in a much more professional manner."

That transformation begins on the very first day, says Gary. "You can see the change in the students, from arriving at college in their day-to-day civilian clothes, to putting the chef's whites on with the Westminster Kingsway College logo, and growing six feet tall," he says. "It's an unbelievable change. The chest puffs out. They have this accentuated sense of determination and ambition that perhaps they didn't have five minutes ago."

who teaches classes in all three year groups. "In the first year we cover the basic science, so we talk about proteins, fats, carbohydrates, what happens to them when they cook, how they're affected by heat, acidity and so on."

"In the second year I then start to teach them in a bit more detail," Rachel continues. "Because as well as an understanding of the knowledge of the science that goes on when they cook, it's very important as chefs, I believe, that they understand how to design an experiment. What you often find in the chef world is that if they want to try something, they approach it like trial and error – try something, it doesn't work, abandon it – rather than a scientific approach of actually doing a very controlled experiment where you change one thing at a time, you have a control, it's done very fair and so on."

"In the third year, they get to use all the slightly more exciting equipment – the sort of things that you would only find in the research laboratories at the Fat Duck, L'Enclume and Restaurant Sat Bains," says Rachel. "So they're basically getting the chance to play with the kind of equipment that the leading chefs in the UK have the opportunity to experiment with."

"This means that they can understand the science behind it and actually use it to innovate to come up with different textures and flavours that they want to try," says Rachel. "And the reason that I think this is very important is that if they want to go down the route of that type of cooking

hosts, for example, wine meat prepared in the boucherie may be served later in one of the college's restaurants. Students aren't just producing food worthy of getting good marks from their lecturers – it has to be food that is suitable for the paying public. It's this that makes these environments absolutely realistic.

In their first year, all students complete the same programme of basic chef training. As they progress through the course, however, they're given the opportunity to specialise in an area that particularly interests them – kitchen and larder, pastry or front of house in the third and final year. This flexibility allows students to develop their skills or personal passions to the fullest.

Whatever the student's specialism, the college's restaurants play an increasingly large role in their experience as they progress through the course. Students spend rotations in The Vincent Rooms Restaurants, the Brasserie and the Escoffier, throughout their time on the Professional Chef Diploma. In the first year they work in the Brasserie as front of house staff, before moving into the kitchen in the second year.

"The good thing about the way that we work it is that they're working alongside third-year students, who will act as their chef de partie," says Gary Hunter. "In specific kitchen areas the third years will have their own section that they're in charge of and they will have a team of two or three second year students who are working on those particular dishes with them."

The exchange of knowledge between peers, supplementing the teaching the students are getting from their lecturers, is central to Westminster Kingsway College's approach – and it's something that continues throughout the Professional Chef Diploma. In the second year, pupils complete a front of house food and beverage service rotation in the Escoffier, the college's fine dining restaurant. In their third and final year, they are permitted to cook here too.

"For students to walk into the Escoffier kitchen, which bears the name of our founding father, is a big experience," says Gary. "It's a tough kitchen to be in as well, because the menu changes on a weekly basis. It's a structured menu – two sets of seven courses, one vegetarian, one meat and fish. It's always a very busy restaurant, everyone wants to come and eat in here and the standards are exceptional."

Those exceptional standards aren't confined to the kitchens, though – there's a strong emphasis on exceptional food and beverage service as well. "Every single student gets a wine qualification, having spent several intensive weeks in the rotation in year two with me," says restaurant service and wine education course leader Veronique Bonnefoy. "Year three students manage the restaurant, the wine cellar and the wine list. They get far more involved with matching

food and wine using their knowledge and experiences from previous years on the course."

The wine qualification which students receive after completing their time with Veronique is just one example of the extra qualifications built into the Professional Chef Diploma. The college works closely with a number of awarding bodies, including City & Guilds, to ensure a broad and thorough curriculum is covered. The Diploma itself is supported and endorsed by the Craft Guild of Chefs.

As students progress through the course, it's not only their cooking and front of house skills that are honed but also their knowledge of how to manage a busy restaurant service. Esher Williams, programme manager, says: "They're learning cocktail skills, barista skills, supervisory skills, management skills, table theatre or Guéridon work, like flambéing at the table – you name it, they can all do it by the end."

One of the main benefits for Westminster Kingsway College's students is the college's strong links with the industry. It's a historical connection, dating back to the college's origins as a training facility set up to provide new employees for London's top hotels and restaurants, and one that has continued to this day. Thanks to these strong vocational links, students are sent out to complete stages, or externships, at some of the capital's top culinary institutions.

"Every one of the first year students will go out into the industry for a minimum of four weeks," says Gary Hunter. "We will send them all to contract catering companies, usually within the London square mile – the City. They work at places such as HSBC, Coutts – some really big banking names with fantastic dining facilities for both their staff and directors."

Externships are built into every level of the Diploma. In the second year, students usually go to top hotels or private clubs, while in their final year they're typically sent to work in Michelin-starred restaurants. Allocating placements is a two-way process – students can ask to work in specific places if they have somewhere in mind.

"Last year we ran all pastry students through the Savoy Hotel pastry kitchens on their work experience," says pastry chef lecturer Andy Whitson. "A lot of these students are destined for good hotels, good restaurants. They will have no problem in finding a good job in their chosen career."

Ultimately, of course, that is the aim of the Professional Chef Diploma – to provide students with the skills and knowledge to secure the job of their dreams in the hospitality and culinary arts industry. First, though, they've got to complete the course, and to do that, they have to pass their exams.

Each year, students have to complete written assessments, as well as a number of practical exams which test their proficiency in the various skills they've gained throughout the course. In the third year, these exams test the particular area of specialty the students have decided to focus on with examiners directly engaged from the industry to mark and judge each student. Essentially, it is the industry mentors who will grade as to whether a student passes the Professional Chef Diploma.

"The chef and pastry final year students have got their white neckerchiefs on at this point, and they are allowed to wear their toques in the third year – the tall chef's hats," says Gary Hunter. "It will be a tough test for these students to achieve the Westminster Kingsway College Professional Chef Diploma and the final examination will scrutinise all of their skills learned over the past three years. The examination for our restaurant service students is judged in the Escoffier, serving people from industry, the people that

they're being judged by, and it really is very intense. Sometimes I look at it and I think 'we're doing this too much' but we're not, because it's exactly the way we've got to be to match the standards of the industry."

"Even at that point, when we've got a table of four or five sommeliers or restaurant managers sitting there, we've got them saying 'OK, have my business card' to the students," says Gary. "It's not unusual for our students to be walking around with three or four different business cards in their back pocket, with three or four different job offers on there."

Mission accomplished, then. But the Professional Chef Diploma doesn't just turn youngsters into first-class hospitality graduates – the culinary stars of tomorrow – but into confident, rounded individuals too.

"It really is good to see them after three years," says programme manager Terry Tinton. "They come in at 16 years old, quite fresh-faced, not knowing hardly anything at all, but by the time they leave here, they can really show what they've learned and go on in industry, and feel comfortable in high-level establishments, whether it's five-star hotels or Michelin starred restaurants."

Wherever Westminster Kingsway College's Professional Chef Diploma graduates end up, they carry the legacy of this great college with them. The course formerly known as the Cookery Technical Day School may have changed since the days of Messrs Salmon, Senn and Kriens but it's still producing some of the very best chefs, patissiers, waiters and restaurant managers in the business.

The Professional Chef Diploma introduces Westminster Kingsway College students to a whole world of new culinary experiences. But for those students who are hungry for even more, the college also offers an unrivalled range of extracurricular activities designed to broaden young minds ever further.

A significant number of these activities fall under the banner of the Westminster Kingsway College Gastronomic Society. All students automatically become members of this club, and any Society events take place outside of study time, with college commitments always taking precedence.

What kind of things does the Society offer to students? Perhaps the most notable is the yearly Gastronomic Tour which, as its title implies, sees students going on foodie trips to far-flung corners of the globe. Past tours have been to places such as India, New York, Barcelona, Germany's Black Forest, Mexico and St Emilion in France.

"We offer them the opportunity to go abroad to travel, to experience different cultures," says programme manager Alexandra Jones. "If they're keen and they're interested, they can take it forward in so many different ways."

Closer to home, the Society also goes on foraging trips in Wales with Yun Hilder of the Mountain Food Company. Whatever the group finds is served with a late lunch meal. The Society also makes trips to Heritage Prime Farm in Dorset, one of the country's premier biodynamic farms, which sees students helping with chores and learning more about the farm's organic and biodynamic approach.

There are smaller trips, too, such as culinary walks of London, where a lecturer shows and explains points of culinary interest to the students, as well as visits to other culinary destinations such as Billingsgate, Smithfield, Spitalfields, New Covent Garden, Rungis, Laverstoke Park Farm and Newlyn Bay.

Another feature of the Society is its 'Culinary Masters Series' of workshops. As part of this, the college has welcomed some of London's most iconic chefs to deliver workshops to students – people such as Giorgio Locatelli, Brett Graham, Andrew Turner, William Curley, Shane Osborn, Ferran Adria and Oliver Rowe.

As Gary Hunter explains, the aim of the Westminster Kingsway College Gastronomic Society is to provide students with experiences that are genuinely inspiring. "It's about adding to the educational process that we have here at the college and giving the students that much more," he says. "We're plugging into the students all the time: 'What do you think of this? How do you feel about that? What does this taste like? What does that smell like? Why have we done it like this? Why have we not done it like that?"

Another huge part of Westminster Kingsway College's extracurricular programme is culinary competitions. For students wishing to take part in competitive cooking events,

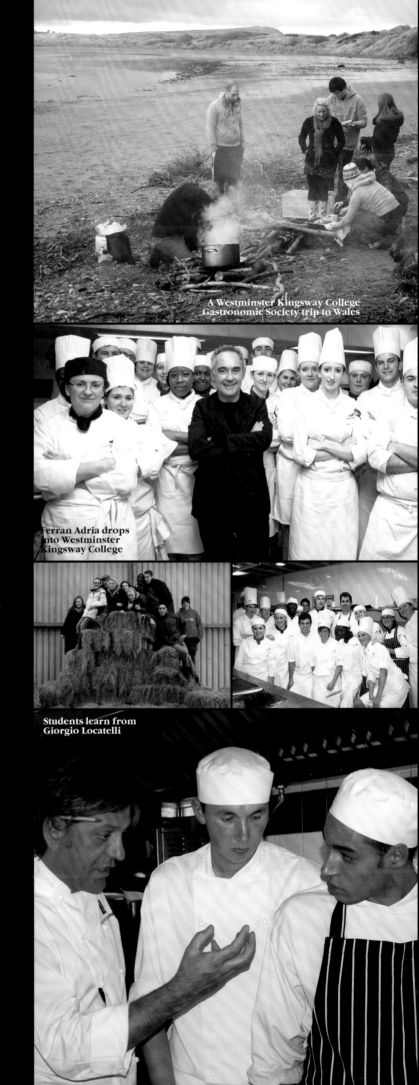

A Westminster Kingsway College Gastronomic Society trip to Wales

Ferran Adria drops into Westminster Kingsway College

Students learn from Giorgio Locatelli

The college has a dedicated group of lecturers – the Westminster Kingsway College Culinary Arts Competition Team – who act as mentors, steering them towards success.

Culinary competitions involve participants cooking or serving a dish or a series of dishes against the clock. According to chef lecturer Jose Souto, this is a great learning environment for students. "It's beneficial for them on many different levels," says Jose, himself an organiser and judge of numerous culinary competitions. "Primarily it teaches them to be organised and to be focused on what they're doing. It also shows them off in a fantastic light to other people."

Gary Hunter agrees. "It's important for our students to be involved in competitions because it's another way of learning in a very acute environment," he says. "You're taking your ingredients and your skills and your equipment, and being judged by people you don't know against the clock, against other students or indeed other people from this industry. And that is an unbelievable learning experience – to be able to cope with that pressure and that stress, but also to be able to learn from what other people are doing, what techniques are out there. They come out of that competition, even if they haven't won, a stronger chef or waiter."

As the old saying goes, it's the taking part that counts, but the Westminster Kingsway College Culinary Arts Competition Team would probably argue that winning isn't half bad either. It's something they're well acquainted with – the team regularly scoops medals and trophies at some of

the biggest competitive events, both nationally and internationally. In 2012, a team of Westminster Kingsway College students, led by chef lecturer Vince Cottam, won one of the most prestigious, the Toque d'Or.

"We have some incredibly successful competition chefs here and that's something that always inspired me as a chef, says Gary. "I've gone out and done competitions across the world and I've learned so much from that environment. It's important that we try and engage the students with that as well to see if they respond to it."

Building and maintaining a successful competition team doesn't come cheap, however, as Gary explains. "I would estimate that to run our competition team each year it takes in excess of £50,000," he says. "But none of it is government funded, none of it is centrally funded, all of it is purely self-produced funding. We do lots of fundraising activities and events and get sponsorship from some brilliant industry friends and sponsors."

Those students lucky enough to have won a place on the full-time Professional Chef Diploma will benefit from an all-encompassing culinary curriculum but Westminster Kingsway College offers its pupils so much more on top of that as well. With things like the Westminster Kingsway College Gastronomic Society and the Westminster Kingsway College Culinary Arts Competition Team, the college offers its students some unforgettable, once-in-a-lifetime learning experiences. And it is experiences like these that turn talented young chefs and waiters into culinary superstars.

An early morning student
trip to Billingsgate Market

"Some of the first year students are lawyers, chemists, who want to learn quickly how to be a professional chef," says chef lecturer Allan Drummond. "The teaching is exactly the same as the Professional Chef Diploma, although we don't teach the front of house modules with them, but we do everything else."

"It's more intense because they're in there for six hours and they're learning everything," says course co-ordinator Ashley Spencer. "Sometimes I would say that the Advanced Diploma is harder to achieve than the Professional Chef Diploma because students are holding down full-time jobs too."

The college also runs more specialised learning programmes, of which perhaps the most notable is the Professional Patisserie Scholarship. "It's the only course which is a scholarship programme for two years for patisserie in the country – nobody else offers it," says Gary Hunter. "Essentially it's like an apprenticeship for pastry chefs. The idea was loosely based on the French system of education. We'll take students who are 16, straight from school, who already know they want to be a pastry chef, and rather than put them through the rigour of a three year stretch studying the Professional Chef Diploma, we'll provide them with a trainee position in a good pastry kitchen in London, with top pastry chefs who are prepared to mentor the students and look after them and support them. They then attend college one day per week."

"The course gives them the basis for everything in patisserie – teaching them the essential skills required to be a top patissier," says pastry chef lecturer Yolande Stanley. "It's up to them how they expand on it, either in the workplace or privately."

That's a statement that could apply to all the culinary arts and hospitality programmes at Westminster Kingsway College. They are courses that provide students – young or old, current chefs and waiters or aspiring ones – with the foundation on which to build. The Professional Chef Diploma may be the college's most famous course but the quality of education on offer here is the same no matter which route students take.

Once students have successfully completed their chosen course, they can go on to graduation, to collect their hard-earned scroll and celebrate with classmates and peers. Then it's onwards again, to a no doubt glittering career in the culinary arts and hospitality industry. Their connection with Westminster Kingsway College doesn't stop there, however. In fact, they're merely entering the next stage of college life by becoming part of its esteemed group of alumni – or, as it's commonly known, the Westminster Kingsway College Family.

Being part of that family has its own special responsibilities, as Gary Hunter explains. "It's about getting the alumni to come back to work with our students in the kitchens or front of house, to work with us on fundraising dinners, to be part of the examinations process, to come back and give presentations and demonstrations to our students, to be a motivational speaker to our students in their first year when they first come in, to try to engage with them and articulate what it feels like to be in their shoes and what the pathway is to becoming a successful student here

at the college. That's the expectation we have of all our alumni: that they're there to help all our current students make that step up to the industry."

"It's like a club really," Gary continues. "I think every ex-student should be part of that without exception. I don't care how busy you are!"

There are massive advantages to being an ex-Westminster Kingsway College student, of course, such as keeping in touch with the college's distinguished – and very well-connected – staff. "Now you've got social media, ex-students are constantly asking us for advice" says chef lecturer Norman Fu. "It's almost like we're their hub for information in the industry. They use us as contacts and we give them references."

As Westminster Kingsway College students become alumni and leave education behind for the world of employment, they have the honour of graduating from arguably the world's greatest School of Hospitality and Culinary Arts. As for the Westminster Kingsway College Family – well, that just keeps getting bigger and better

"Completing the whole course with top marks and distinctions was a first for me so it felt great. It made me grow up fast, understand the wider industry and gave me confidence."
– Jamie Oliver

Past Masters

Today, Westminster Kingsway College is probably best known for its glittering roster of former students. The college is a true star-maker, the springboard for the successful careers of countless celebrity chefs.

It's not just about the famous faces, though. The college has also produced graduates who, while they may not be household names, have gone on to outstanding careers in the hospitality industry, whether working in top-flight hotels and first-rate restaurants around the globe or setting up their own ventures. Many have earned awards, Michelin stars and even MBEs. There are those who've used their experience at Westminster Kingsway College to set up colleges of their

own. There are those who returned to the college as staff, following in the footsteps of their beloved mentors. And there are even some Westminster Kingsway College couples, classmates whose romance blossomed at the college.

The one thing all ex-Westminster Kingsway College students have in common, however, is love for their alma mater. Each of them acknowledges the debt they owe to the college, and the role it played in helping them get where they are today.

Here, some of Westminster Kingsway College's most prominent alumni share their memories of the college, along with more than a few funny stories...

Jamie Oliver

Arguably the most famous of all Westminster Kingsway College's ex-students, Jamie Oliver is an international star. Since he burst onto our screens on the BBC's The Naked Chef, he's rarely been off them, with TV shows such as Jamie At Home and Jamie's 30-Minute Meals all proving to be huge hits. He's also put the skills he gained at Westminster Kingsway College to good use as a successful restaurateur, a bestselling author and a passionate campaigner on food-related issues. For all his triumphs, though, he's never forgotten his roots.

"It was fantastic," says Jamie of his time at Westminster Kingsway College. "I loved how multi-cultural it was; it seemed like there were students from every country in the world."

"Completing the whole course with top marks and distinctions was a first for me so it felt great," he says. "It made me grow up fast, understand the wider industry and gave me confidence."

What does Jamie think makes Westminster Kingsway College so special?

"So many things, but obviously culturally it's a big old grand college that has the respect of the industry," he says. "It has a great reputation in one of the best food cities in the world."

Diversity, history, location – just some of the things that Jamie says puts Westminster Kingsway College ahead of the pack. But as the man himself says, there's fun to be had as well.

"We had loads of laughs... not all publishable!" he says. "The chef lecturers were great, and would send us young chefs on a lot of errands to collect a bottle of Chateaubriand, or to the stores for tartan food colouring."

Jamie's TV programmes continue to be shown in syndication around the globe, and his latest book, Jamie's Money Saving Meals, is another bestseller so clearly his status as the UK's most recognisable chef isn't going to change any time soon. But he remains grateful to Westminster Kingsway College for the role it played in helping to launch that stellar career. It is, he says, "the best catering college in the country."

Ben Murphy

"My time at college was a highlight of my life. Going from not knowing how to hold a knife, to competing in competitions in the second year and then graduating with a distinction diploma in the third was remarkable."

Ben Murphy is proof of what Westminster Kingsway College can help students achieve if they're willing to put the work in. It goes without saying that young Ben is willing to put that work in, and then some.

After graduating with top grades in 2010, Ben landed a job with Pierre Koffmann at London's famous Berkeley hotel. From there he moved to France to work at Les Pres d'Eugenie, the restaurant of renowned chef and inventor of cuisine minceur Michael Guerard. In between, he won a gold medal at WorldSkills London 2011 and was crowned National Young Chef of the Year and the UK's Spanish Chef of the Year.

Ben's clearly talented but he says his success is all down to Westminster Kingsway College and one chef lecturer in particular.

"If I had any doubts, I could always bounce back on chef Norman Fu for guidance," he says. "Westminster Kingsway College is special because of the staff and everyone who put in the effort to get the best out of all the students."

Ainsley Harriott

Ainsley Harriott has been a charismatic presence on our television screens for the best part of 20 years. His larger-than-life personality and flamboyant cooking style, showcased during stints as presenter of the BBC's Can't Cook, Won't Cook and Ready, Steady, Cook, have made him a much-loved household name. But Ainsley's journey to stardom began at Westminster Kingsway College, where he studied in the 1970s.

"I learnt so much about the history of food," he says. "The best thing was the camaraderie – people in the same position as you."

These days, Ainsley is an internationally-renowned cook, with a range of branded products and bestselling books to his name. But he hasn't forgotten the role Westminster

Kingsway College played in helping him get there.

"I'm often back there giving awards," he says. "It's great to know that the standards are maintained, to know the quality of the teaching staff is still high."

With more TV projects in the pipeline, Ainsley's status as a household name doesn't look set to change anytime soon. To his old teachers, though, he's more famous for fooling around in class, in more ways than one...

"I remember one of the chef lecturers catching me in the fridge snogging a girl once," he says. "I only went in for some watercress!"

Bev Puxley

The majority of Westminster Kingsway College alumni have fond memories of their time at the college but it's safe to say Bev Puxley has more than most. Because he's not just an ex-student, he's an ex-head of department as well.

Bev studied the Professional Chef Diploma from 1951 to 1953, winning the Isidore Salmon prize for top student in the process. After a career including stints at Claridge's and teaching in South Devon, in 1980 he responded to an advert and was appointed Head of Professional Cookery, before becoming Head of the School of Hotel, Catering & Tourism from 1987 to 1995.

Bev's 18 years at Westminster Kingsway College have been a huge influence on him. His son's second name is Vincent, after Jean Vincent, another former Head of Professional Cookery. And the college played another important part in his life too...

"I had been sent to the pantry to polish silver as a result of committing some horrendous gastronomic disaster. Perhaps my carrots jardinière were cut just a millimetre too long. Whilst there I noticed a young hotel operations student scraping plate waste into a bucket. The bucket was getting very full. My first words to her were "May I empty your bucket for you?" "Oh, yes, thank you", she replied.

"I returned to the student refectory and told my friend, Tony Sellar, that I had just met the girl I intended to marry. "I bet you twenty five quid you don't", said Tony. That young lady, Pam Goodwin, became my wife in 1956. In spite of us still going strong today, Tony still owes me the money!"

Although now retired, Bev is Master of the Worshipful Company of Cooks and serves on 16 industry-related committees, including as an independent adviser to the Food Services School at the RLC (Royal Logistics Corps). But it's his time at Westminster Kingsway College that he remains most proud of.

"Anyone who has worked in any capacity for the college knows that they are merely passing occupants or caretakers at an institution which is bigger than all of them," he says. "Westminster Kingsway College is a national treasure."

Chris Bailey

Chris Bailey is one of many ex-Westminster Kingsway College students who have not only worked in a Michelin star restaurant but also earned one themselves. After graduating from the college in 2002 and working in London and Spain, he opened The Black Rat in Winchester and it wasn't long before his modern, seasonal British food got the nod from the prestigious Michelin Guide.

Chris is now working on a series of pop-up events called the Interim Table. Like many other alumni, though, he looks back on his time at Westminster Kingsway College with fondness: "I enjoyed learning the classics in the main kitchen, as well as having great fun with other students."

Fabio Arcari

After working at eateries with three Michelin stars, Fabio Arcari is now a company director of a chain of family-run Italian delicatessen restaurants. However, before all that, he needed a catering education, and Westminster Kingsway College was the place he chose to get one.

"It had the best reputation, and was the most recognised college for the hospitality industry," says Fabio, who graduated in 2003.

Fabio's time at Westminster Kingsway College set him on the path to success. But he has his fair share of funny stories about his college days too.

"I remember carefully constructing a four-yolk egg with my friend, by pouring three yolks into an already-cracked egg and waiting for the pastry chef to come round before cracking it fully in front of him," he says. "His utter amazement was great. He claimed in 40 years in the industry he'd never seen such a thing! We never had the heart to tell him it was a joke after the excitement that he showed."

Fernando & Kristy Stovell

Husband-and-wife team Fernando and Kristy Stovell are proving a formidable foodie duo, with successful stints at top establishments being followed by the opening of their own restaurant in 2012. They have Westminster Kingsway College to thank for their marriage as well as their career: the pair met at the college.

"We have been working together pretty much since we left college," says Fernando. "We believe we are a very good team and complement each other."

The couple graduated from Westminster Kingsway College in 2000. Fernando, originally from Mexico, worked at restaurants including the two Michelin-starred Eric Chavot at The Capital before becoming joint head chef at The Wellington Club with Kristy, who hails from New Zealand. They moved together to The Cuckoo Club, before opening their own venture, Stovell's, in Chobham, Surrey.

"We can proudly say that things are going very good and we're pleased about the recognition we both have been getting in such a short period of opening," says Fernando. "We've been voted number 42 best restaurant outside London by Square Meal, we've got five points on the Good Food Guide and two rosettes."

A Westminster Kingsway College power couple? You'd better believe it.

Geoff Acott

Having been a chef at The Ritz, the Institute of Directors, the Army Catering Corps and the Ministry of Defence, Geoff Acott's culinary career has been both successful and diverse. His latest achievement, however, is undoubtedly the icing on the cake.

"I have just been awarded the MBE for services to the catering industry in the 2013 Queen's Birthday Honours list," says Geoff. "I am obviously thrilled and delighted."

Geoff graduated from Westminster Kingsway College in 1964. He currently serves as National Treasurer for the Craft Guild of Chefs, advising the Chairman and Committee of Management on financial matters. But it was Geoff's time at Westminster Kingsway College that was the catalyst for his long and varied career.

"It inspired a passion for the craft, a love of ingredients and a fierce desire to advance my personal skills and attributes," he says.

What does Geoff think makes Westminster Kingsway College so special?

"Without doubt it is the people, both students and the faculty," he says. "They all have the passion too."

Geoffrey Smeddle

In 1993, Geoffrey Smeddle wanted to enrol at catering college, and there was only one place he was going to go.

"Westminster Kingsway College was considered, even then, to be the best," he says. "Being progressive in outlook and instilling discipline from day one was always important then, and those values are still there."

During his time at Westminster Kingsway College, Geoffrey was something of a star student.

"At the end of my second year I won the Iwan Kriens award for best student," he says.

Geoffrey's diligence at college paid off. He has gone on to enjoy an award-winning career.

"After leaving I started as a commis chef at The Grill Room at The Cafe Royal under Herbert Berger. It had one Michelin star and was like my ultimate finishing school," he says. "Today I am chef patron of The Peat Inn. We hold one Michelin star and seven out of ten in The Good Food Guide. My small team is dedicated beyond belief. I have guys who have been with me three years and four years, so we achieve great consistency and enjoy a relaxed atmosphere. Of course, this is not the same as a relaxed attitude!"

Henry Herbert

The name Henry Herbert might not mean that much to people at the moment, but his pseudonym certainly will: he's a Fabulous Baker Brother.

Along with his sibling Tom, the younger Herbert is the star of the popular Channel 4 TV show. Before the small screen came calling, however, Henry was a Westminster Kingsway College student from 2005 to 2008.

"I first heard of Westminster Kingsway College from a Jamie Oliver cook book. I love its history and how it prides itself on being the best in Britain for education, contacts and work ethic," he says. "I wanted to be challenged and be right at the heart of cooking in central London."

After graduating, Henry worked at the Prince of Wales gastropub in Putney, before becoming head chef at The Coach & Horses in Clerkenwell. It was here that he first caught the eye of television bosses, gaining an invite to appear on BBC One's Great British Menu. Since then, he's been a very busy man.

"I currently work with my family business Hobbs House Bakery, particularly their retail and butchery," says Henry.

"I'm also heading out to America with my brother Tom to film a series for Discovery Channel TLC. We have signed a four-year contract, which is amazing and terrifying but the thought of travelling around America eating and cooking food is a dream come true."

What is Henry's tip for fledgling cooks looking to follow in his footsteps? Start at Westminster Kingsway College.

"If any budding young chef asks for advice with learning to cook I always say go to catering college and, if you can get in, apply for Westminster Kingsway College," he says. "There is no better start for a young chef."

Ian Nottage

If the walls of Westminster Kingsway College could talk, they'd have some tales to tell. Ian Nottage, a student from 1980 to 1983 and 1986 to 1988, has one of his own.

"We were preparing roast chicken classically garnished. We had prepared the game chips, roast gravy, bread sauce and had a mid-lesson break prior to presenting our dishes," he says. "As we were chatting we started grazing on the freshly prepared game chips and before we realized it we had eaten the lot.

"Rather than getting a blasting from our tutor, the formidable Mrs Beeby, we sent one of our number down to the local corner shop to buy crisps to replace them with. We just had time to decant the crisps onto the silver flats we were to present our chickens on and dispose of the packets.

"In due time, we all had to present our dishes to Chef Beeby to be evaluated. She tasted one of my game chips and pulled a face: 'To the best of my knowledge, Mr Nottage, neither

Practical Cookery, Larousse Gastronomique nor Le Repertoire ever called for them to be cheese and onion flavour!'"

Despite the game chip incident, Ian graduated from Westminster Kingsway College, and now works as chef director for Reynolds Catering Supplies. But he still retains strong links with the college, a place he's proud to be associated with.

"When I go back for industry events or for judging it feels like stepping back in time, especially if you get a whiff of a stock pot or a bouquet garni," he says. "I think what really makes the college so special are the lecturers. They are amazing. They always go the extra mile for the good of the students and the college as a whole."

Joseph Seeletso

Joseph's journey to culinary stardom has been just that: a journey. He was born in Botswana into a royal family and has gone on to cook at hotels and restaurants in his home country, Poland and Sweden, where he is a regular guest chef cooking for King Carl XVI Gustaf and Queen Silvia. His journey began in London at Westminster Kingsway College in 1995.

"I remember I arrived at what was then Westminster College from the airport after an 11-hour flight from Botswana," says Joseph. "My first contact was with chef Shoesmith. He ushered me straight to the International team, who helped me with finding accommodation and getting around London.

Throughout his time at Westminster Kingsway College, Joseph was a high flyer.

"My first achievement was winning the Southern regional Toque d'Or competition in Earl's Court with my teammate Megat Mokhatar and then second at the 1998 Toque d'Or finals, beating close to 140 teams from all over the UK," he says. "And once when I was doing a job placement at the Marriott Grosvenor Square I remember making a Caesar salad with the chef de partie for Michael Jackson!"

These days, Joseph is a celebrity chef and TV star based in Poland where he is currently the judge of Polish Top Chef, but he's still immensely proud of his time in London.

"I feel very special because I was the first person from Botswana to get the Westminster Kingsway College Professional Chef's Diploma."

Louise & Lucien Bintcliffe

It seems Westminster Kingsway College is just as adept at matchmaking as it is at producing top chefs. Louise and Lucien Bintcliffe are another couple who met at the college and now they share a workplace as well as a home.

"We are both sous chefs at The Royal Horseguards Hotel,"

says Louise. "Lucien works in the One Twenty One Two Restaurant for head chef Ryan Mattheson and I work in the hotel's pastry kitchen for head pastry chef Joanne Todd.

"We worked together a lot at Westminster Kingsway College so we knew we could do it before we signed up!" she continues. "We also have strict rules: leave work at the door and home at the staff entrance."

The pair studied at Westminster Kingsway College between 2005 and 2008. Between them they gained some incredible experience, both during and immediately after their time at college, including competition wins and stints at top restaurants and hotels. But without their Westminster Kingsway College education, says Lucien, they wouldn't be where they are today.

"It's one of only a handful of colleges that have realistic working environments that are genuinely busy and serving modern or current dishes," he says. "The teachers are fantastic as well. They are always there for advice, even when you've left."

Michael Nadell

It goes without saying that students get a superb culinary education at Westminster Kingsway College but it's by no means plain sailing, as Michael Nadell once discovered.

"Rene Le Prince ran the vegetable, eggs and farinaceous section, a giant of a man with enormous hands," says Michael, a student from 1963 to 1965.

"At exam time, I had to make a cream of carrot soup and Pomme Anna. I got the potato dish into the oven and then made and finished my soup. At 11.30, one hour before service, I presented my soup to Rene and he promptly poured it down the sink.

"'What was wrong with it?' I asked. 'You didn't even taste it!' 'You finished too early,' he replied. 'Now make your soup again and remember service starts in one hour.' After all of that, he gave me nine and a half out of ten and said I would have got ten but for the soup going down the drain!"

Undeterred, Michael went on to win gold medals in competitions such as Hotelympia during his time at the college. After working as head pastry chef in five-star hotels and teaching part-time at a local college, he set up Nadell Patisserie, which today provides quality cakes and pastries to the industry. As for Michael's college days, they continue to influence his work.

"My years at Westminster Kingsway College gave me a wonderful grounding for the years ahead," says Michael. "I still use many of my college recipes in my daily work."

Paul Gregory

When Paul Gregory originally enrolled at Westminster Kingsway College in 1986, it was on an electronics course. But Paul's dyslexia made him decide to change tack.

"It just wasn't me," he says. "I wanted something more hands-on."

The practical path he chose was cooking, first on a cooking course in 1992, then a patisserie course in 1998. It was a career move that paid off: he's now one of the country's finest chocolatiers.

Paul served time in Michelin-starred restaurants, before setting up Paul Wayne Gregory Ltd, his own company that produces bespoke chocolate artistry for clients all over the world.

Paul's successes in the industry are largely thanks to his natural inquisitiveness about food, something that blossomed during his time at Westminster Kingsway College, much to the chagrin of his lecturers.

"Gary Hunter always used to say 'Any questions? Apart from Paul!'" he says. "But having that curiosity put me in the position that I'm in now," he continues. "The theory side is important; you wouldn't discuss the properties of gluten or flour in a restaurant but you learn it on the course. Once you know it, it becomes part of you. It's only years later that I actually appreciated it."

Paul Walsh

Paul Walsh's love of cooking started at an early age. Wanting to hone his skills, he started looking for colleges and one name cropped up again and again.

"I kept hearing 'Westminster, Westminster, Westminster'," says Paul. "If that was the best, that's where I was going to go."

Paul enrolled at the college in 2002, and after graduating in 2005 went on to a stellar career working with Gordon Ramsay at the Savoy Grill and later the three Michelin-starred Royal Hospital Road. He then served as executive chef at 28-50 Wine Workshop & Kitchen, which now has three outlets in London. Next, he's planning to open a restaurant of his own with celebrity chef Jason Atherton.

Having risen through the ranks to the very top, Paul's now in a position to pass on his knowledge to the next generation, knowledge he gained at Westminster Kingsway College.

"One of our chef lecturers, Bob Salt, used to say, "I will, we will, you will", meaning I'll show you how to do a dish, then we'll do one together, then you'll do one on your own," says Paul.

"I still do that with the young chefs who come to me."

Raj Sharma

Raj Sharma's time at Westminster Kingsway College changed his life. Having travelled from India to study at the college, he went on to work for famous chefs and cook for celebrities, world leaders and royals. Now, inspired by Westminster Kingsway College, he's setting up a college of his own in his native India.

"My dream was to open up a new college," he says. "It has taken a lot of planning but I've used what I learned at Westminster Kingsway College."

Raj's dream has come true in the form of the Oxford International College of Hospitality and Business Management, in his native India. As its title suggests, it will offer HND and NVQ courses in the hospitality and business fields, with the first students being accepted in 2014.

During his time at Westminster Kingsway College (1998-2003), Raj was a star pupil, gaining several qualifications and taking part in many competitions. After working in top establishments around the world, he became executive chef of News International (now News UK) in 2011. Now he's hoping his latest venture will prove just as inspirational as his alma mater. What is it, does he think, that makes Westminster Kingsway College so special?

"Absolutely everything," he says. "The supporting staff, the amazing facilities and the constant change, every year they bring new things."

Rosalind Parsk

To say Rosalind Parsk is talented is an understatement to say the least. She's been a high flyer ever since her Westminster Kingsway College days.

"We were encouraged to compete in competitions, and I won the most medals in my year so I was sent to Las Vegas for two weeks to work in The Golden Nugget Hotel and Casino. I had the most amazing time," says Rosalind, who was a student from 2001 to 2004. "To top off my whole Westminster Kingsway College experience I got a distinction and the highest mark out of the whole year."

During her time at the college, Rosalind took part in a ten-episode TV programme called Yes Chef!, which saw six Westminster Kingsway College students competing for a £500 prize by being sent to work in top London restaurants. Yes, you guessed it, Rosalind won.

After graduating, Rosalind's culinary prowess landed her a commis chef role at the Connaught Hotel under Angela Hartnett. After three years, she made the move to Dubai to work for Gary Rhodes and now she's Chef de Cuisine at PierChic.

"I love working and living in Dubai. It has the sun, the sea, sand and the lifestyle... what more could you want?"

Russell Bateman

Russell Bateman turned his Westminster Kingsway College education into a successful restaurant career, with stints at places such as Chapter One and Petrus paving the way for his current role as head chef at Collette's at The Grove. On a recent trip back to his old college, he discovered the standards that propelled him to the top are still firmly in place.

"I saw the exact reason why it's so special: hospitality. That's the business we're in and that's what it's all about," says Russell, a student from 1996 to 1998. "When I arrived I was greeted with a lovely smile and given a full tour. Nothing was too much to ask. True hospitality can be taught but it's also something that is catching."

"The other thing I noticed was the college's progressiveness," he continues. "It's moving with the times."

Russell is equally impressed by the next generation of Westminster Kingsway College students. "Recently I had the good fortune to work with some Westminster Kingsway College students on a 'Passion to Inspire' Dinner at the Novotel in Hammersmith," he says. "Their attitudes towards the event and work were exemplary. No job was too big or too menial and they approached all tasks with the same vigour.

"I'm proud to say that I went to the same college as those guys," he says. "And one day those students will be at the top of our industry, thanks to the foundation given to them by Westminster Kingsway College."

Selin Kiazim

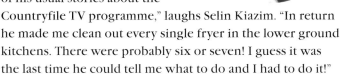

"On the last day of college I remember a few of us having a laugh and joke with chef lecturer, Vince Cottam. I told him to 'bore off.' He was probably telling us one of his usual stories about the Countryfile TV programme," laughs Selin Kiazim. "In return he made me clean out every single fryer in the lower ground kitchens. There were probably six or seven! I guess it was the last time he could tell me what to do and I had to do it!"

Selin Kiazim left Westminster Kingsway College in 2008, to a career that's seen her working in restaurants and trying out her modern Turkish food on the public at a series of pop-up events. Now she has taken things to the next level with the opening of a permanent space in Haggerston, but she acknowledges the role the college played in her getting there.

"For me the most special thing were the lecturers," she says. "They taught me an incredible amount and ensured I had fun with it but they also pushed me as far as they could to get the best out of me. I think the college has built up an amazing reputation for themselves and they continue to uphold that through their staff."

Tom Egerton

For many Westminster Kingsway College students, cooking competitions are a big part of college life, affording the opportunity to show off your skills somewhere other than a restaurant or classroom. In 2005, Tom Egerton and his classmates took part in one of the most prestigious, the Toque d'Or, and won.

"Winning was great," he says. "We had all put a lot of time and effort getting everything ready. We had a great team and lots of support from the college. The winning prize included a trip to America, which was amazing."

After graduating in 2008, Tom worked for celebrity chef Gary Rhodes, before moving to Dubai, where he currently serves as senior executive sous chef of the Grosvenor House Hotel. Clearly, he's a man with an excellent work ethic, something which was drummed into him at Westminster Kingsway College.

"I ended up with the top marks in my year which I was very proud of," says Tom. "I believe my parents were very proud of what I had achieved but only really understood what I did a few years later. They could never work out why I worked such long hours!"

Stephen Gadd

Stephen Gadd studied a Hospitality and Catering course at Westminster Kingsway College in 2001, before enrolling on the Professional Chef Diploma in 2002. A decade on, he still reminisces about his time at the college.

"There are so many reasons why I enjoyed Westminster Kingsway College," he says. "The college was a very professional place and instilled in you great discipline but with the freedom to learn and create, which I think is a hard mix to achieve.

"I still talk about college. A fellow chef who I work with at the moment has just completed a pastry course and I love chatting away about college stories, lecturers and general college life with him," says Stephen, who has worked in a number of Michelin starred restaurants since leaving Westminster Kingsway College. "I am best friends with people I went to college with. I have cooked with ex-students in restaurants and pubs and our bond was always strong as we always had the college in common.

"I always say that my four years at Westminster Kingsway College was fantastic. If you're young and thinking about becoming a chef then I think there is only one option: sign up to Westminster Kingsway College, cross your fingers and hope you get a place!"

Darrel Wilde

John Burton-Race. Raymond Blanc. Gary Rhodes. Three famous Michelin starred chefs and Darrel Wilde has worked for them all. Now he's head chef at the four star Cumberland Hotel in London but his culinary journey began at Westminster Kingsway College.

"I loved every single day I was at the college and couldn't wait to get back there each Monday morning," says Darrel, a student from 1995 to 1997. "My proudest achievement at Westminster Kingsway College was winning the Worshipful Company of Cooks Young Chef of the Year in 1996. This was a tremendous feeling, knowing that I had put a lot of work into it, and not only did I feel proud but I know that I made a lot of lecturers proud who had given me a lot of their time and believed in me."

A big part of the Westminster Kingsway College experience is the social side of things, with many students making friends for life at the college. That was certainly the case for Darrel; he's now godfather to former classmate Marvin Jones's son.

Darrel and Marvin are regularly back at their old stomping ground, taking part in various functions and helping lecturers to mark end of year exams. For this proud alumnus, Westminster Kingsway College is a truly special place.

"The history that surrounds the college and its legacy will go on forever," says Darrel. "I'm just proud that I was a small piece of that history."

William Horswill

There are, of course, many reasons for a young chef to want to study at Westminster Kingsway College. For William Horswill, however, it was all because of the college's most famous son.

"The main reason I chose to study there was because of Jamie Oliver. I'd heard him mention it in a magazine article," says William, who graduated in 2006 with a Distinction in the Professional Chef Diploma. "The reason I got into cooking was watching him on TV. I think that's the same with a lot of chefs my age, although they probably wouldn't admit it!"

William followed in his hero's footsteps to become a top Westminster Kingsway College student. He received an award for Best Student in his final year before embarking on a successful restaurant career. After stints at Michelin starred establishments around London, he became head chef of the trendy Burger & Lobster, noted for its main course menu consisting solely of... burger and lobster. There are now a further three outlets in the capital. There are also with plans to expand further, and William has risen to the rank of executive head chef, overseeing all of them. His biggest influence on his work, though, is still Westminster Kingsway College.

"It's a little bit of a cliché but I still use the same techniques I learned at the college" he says. "Even though Burger &

Lobster is a mono-product operation, we still employ the same discipline, the same mentality; they're all fundamental."

John Lawson

Many ex-Westminster Kingsway College students say that the thing that makes the college stand out from the rest is its amazing lecturers. John Lawson, a student from 1999 to 2002, would certainly agree.

"I enjoyed learning from the most knowledgable lecturers there can possibly be!" he says. "Especially Chef Innes – he was my favourite. Completely in love with food and the most knowledgable chef I've come across in my career thus far."

And what a career it's been. Having discovered a love for cooking while helping out at his father's local pub as a youngster, John enrolled at Westminster Kingsway College and from there went on to work for top chefs Raymond Blanc, Daniel Boulud and Gordon Ramsay, in both the UK and the US.

After a move down under, John is now executive chef of No.8 at Crown, a luxury hotel in Melbourne, Australia, but he still has much praise for his alma mater.

"This college prepares you in the best possible way for a career in the hospitality industry," he says. "It covers all areas and has a great blend of practical and theory."

Sarah Frankland

As head pâtissier for William Curley, the renowned chocolatier and pâtissier, Sarah Frankland is responsible for recruiting new employees, amongst many other tasks, and there's one thing that makes that job a little easier.

"Whenever I receive CVs for jobs, if they have trained at Westminster Kingsway College they go to the top of the pile!" she says. "Seven out of ten pastry chefs at William Curley trained at the college."

Sarah studied at Westminster Kingsway College between 2004 and 2006 on the professional patisserie scholarship. She had been sponsored by top chef Angela Hartnett for a place on the course, which combines classroom work with work experience. In Sarah's case this was with Angela at London's five-star Connaught Hotel. From there she moved to William Curley, where she has now been for a six and a half years.

Still young, Sarah's career trajectory continues ever upwards, fired by her passion for pastry. And, as she explains, she has Westminster Kingsway College to thank for inspiring that passion in the first place.

"I decided to join Westminster Kingsway College because I had attended a one-day course taken by Gary Hunter, learning to make a Sacher Torte and chocolate bon bons," she says. "I enjoyed it so much I knew I wanted to learn patisserie."

Paul Gayler

What Paul Gayler hasn't done in the hospitality industry frankly isn't worth doing. He is the acclaimed author of 21 cook books, a respected television chef, a dedicated charity fundraiser and, of course, a talented cook, having served at some of the world's finest hotels. He was also honoured with an MBE too, awarded in recognition of his services to the industry and his charity work.

Quite a CV.

Paul is now Executive Chef at London's five-star Lanesborough Hotel, but it was his time at Westminster Kingsway College, from 1978 to 1980 studying an Advanced Cookery course, that focused his talent and kick-started his rise to the top.

"The time I spent at the college really set the standards I wanted to achieve in my career, and stands me in good stead up to the present day," says Paul. "Westminster Kingsway College has a fine reputation and anyone on a course can take heart that it is a good indication of good solid training, and well respected in the industry."

The other thing that Paul remembers about his time at Westminster Kingsway College is the fabulous lecturers, in particular his favourite, Freddie Woods.

"I loved Freddie, he pulled you down to earth," says Paul. "He was fair and complimentary, but also firm and abrupt when he needed to be. I really respected him for that. I owe him a lot!

"I remember on one pre-exam test, I thought my consommé was a triumph. The garnish for the consommé was chervil and tarragon floating in the clear amber soup. I proudly took it to the hot pass, placed it before Freddie and thought 'he will be pleased with this.'

"On returning to my work station, I heard a scream from Freddie: 'What's this Gayler? Bloody Hyde Park Corner?!' I think he felt I had overdone the green herb garnish!"

Julian Tworek

Westminster Kingsway College alumni come from every corner of the globe, and go on to work in every corner of the globe as well. Take Julian Tworek for example, he's now the Executive Chef at the Westin Hotel in Kuala Lumpur, Malaysia.

It's the latest stage in a glittering career for this young chef. After completing the AVCE Advanced Hotel & Restaurant Management course in 2003, Julian spent a further three years at Westminster Kingsway College studying the Professional Chef Diploma. From there, he worked at Michelin starred restaurants with some of the best chefs in the business, including Alain Ducasse and Helene Darroze.

Great as these mentors were, however, Julian still considers his teachers at Westminster Kingsway College a huge influence.

"A great team with many skills put together in one building," says Julian. "We picked their brains as much as we could."

For chefs, hard work, determination and ambition are part of the job description. For Julian, that's a lesson he learned at Westminster Kingsway College, and it's one that set him on the path to success.

"You realise that you need to sacrifice a large part of your 20s never stopping and climbing as high as possible but in the end it is worth it," he says. "Looking back I can say I was happy to be there and proud to state that I trained there."

Sophie Wright

When will Westminster Kingsway College produce 'the next Jamie Oliver'?

In Sophie Wright, they may already have. This rising star has an ever-growing media profile, with a column in Great British Food Magazine, a spot on the panel of BBC Radio 4's The Kitchen Cabinet and a string of TV appearances already under her belt. And that's before mentioning her three award-winning cookery books.

Sophie completed her Professional Chef's Diploma at Westminster Kingsway College in 2006 and she has maintained strong ties to the college ever since.

"Westminster Kingsway College is an institution and the college that all colleges strive to be," she says. "It's held in high acclaim worldwide, and for very, very good

reason! It still feels like home when I walk through the doors and will always hold a very special place in my heart."

In between her media work, Sophie's bread and butter – pardon the pun – is her company, Sophie Wright Catering. It's a business that has gone from strength to strength, something she also credits to Westminster Kingsway College.

"I learnt so much whilst at the college," she says. "It gave me the confidence to strive and to always work hard and trust what I had been taught."

Staff

For all its illustrious history, its gifted students and the famous faces that have sprung forth from its doors, the thing that Westminster Kingsway College is truly built on is its staff. The college's first lecturers and founding fathers were some of the most iconic figures in the hospitality industry, and that legacy has continued through to this day.

Between them, Westminster Kingsway College's current team have worked at some of the best Michelin-starred restaurants, five-star hotels and top-flight institutions in the country, and indeed across the globe. They've won major awards and scooped prizes in some of the culinary world's most prestigious competitions. And now they're passing on their skills and knowledge to the next generation as lecturers at the UK's oldest and most renowned school of hospitality and culinary arts.

The current Westminster Kingsway College teaching team

Gary Hunter

Culinary Arts &
Hospitality Management Team

In 1910, the school that would eventually become Westminster Kingsway College was founded thanks to the vision of people such as Auguste Escoffier and Isidore Salmon. Today, it operates under the leadership of its head of culinary arts, hospitality and food and beverage service, **Gary Hunter**.

"It's a heavy responsibility, really, to head up that whole team with the history the college has, but the good thing about our department is that we develop and increase our curriculum on a yearly basis, so we expand and grow together rather than remain the same or shrink," he says. "The team is everything. I know it's a cliché, but it is."

After a career in Michelin-starred restaurants, prestigious country house hotels and a stage as head of a pastry team in Pakistan, Gary came to Westminster Kingsway College in the late 1990s, initially as a pastry chef lecturer. The college he found, however, was a deep institution founded on the 'Westminster Way' dictum.

"I think when I first came here, it was bewildering being part of a team that was such a large traditional institution," he says. "They were facing up to new challenges of curriculum transformation – there were some big changes in further education at that time. You can operate in one of two ways: you can either go into decline and cut your cloth accordingly, or you can say 'you know what? Here's an opportunity to make us a lot more fit for purpose, and to realign ourselves with what our true core values are and build.'"

Gary was quickly promoted to be head of the pastry team. Soon afterwards, he was appointed to his current position as head of hospitality and culinary arts. From the outset, he resolved to change things for the better of the college and hospitality industry.

"It was just a case of starting all over again and seeing what the new educational era was all about, planning a strategy and a blueprint for what we wanted to achieve, and

The management team
(l-r): Alexandra Jones,
Gary Hunter, Terry
Tinton, Esher Williams

As **Terry Tinton** explains, it's a challenging but rewarding role.

"My job really is the day to day maintaining and managing of the team, and working on product development and programmes for next year, organising and developing new commercial courses for the entire team," he says. "Part-time professional chef courses as well – I co-ordinate all the teams and students for that – and I manage the International Patisserie and International Culinary Diplomas, which are the intensive 24-week courses that we deliver."

Terry, whose background is in Michelin starred restaurants and top-flight hotels, as well as a stint at the House of Commons, is clearly a very busy man. But like Gary, he has a determination to make Westminster Kingsway College the best college it can be, and to foster a culture of constant improvement here.

"It's about changing the way that people see colleges and the sort of work that we do; not resting on our laurels," he says. "What we've found in the past is that employers and leading industry members have an overall view of colleges and what they do on a day-to-day basis, but what we've encouraged over the years is an open-door policy, especially for judging and master classes and in using social media, so that they can see what we're actually doing. It really does raise the profile of the culinary arts team. It's about having that brand that we're proud of and taking it forward for the future."

For programme manager **Esher Williams**, it's this commitment to excellence that sets Westminster Kingsway College apart.

Despite her relative youth, Esher has more experience of the college than most. She's an ex-student, graduating with a qualification in Hospitality Management with Tourism in 2005. During her time at the college, Esher was a successful competition member, being part of a Westminster Kingsway College team that won the prestigious Toque d'Or event in 2005. This success was the springboard for a glittering career, including time at the Savoy Hotel, L'Ortolan and

Terry Tinton

Alexandra Jones

Esher Williams

Heston Blumenthal's Fat Duck. Esher's connection with Heston has seen her appear alongside the famous chef on his TV programmes. But even a burgeoning television career couldn't keep her from wanting to return to Westminster Kingsway College.

"I love the college, I thoroughly enjoyed my time here and I was always keen to keep connected and help out in any way I could," she says. "The culture, I think, is very special here. I believe it's the best place in the country."

For programme manager **Alexandra Jones**, having ex-students like Esher back as members of staff is the perfect illustration of the quality of teaching at Westminster Kingsway College.

"It's so gratifying when you get a tap on the shoulder and there they are, and they're married, they've got children and they remember you and they're still in the business, and they've recommended people to come or they want to come back and become lecturers," she says. "You realise you've got it right when they want to come back and teach."

Alexandra joined the college in 1996. She's held practically every lecturer position there is, progressing up through the ranks to her current role. Alongside her duties as programme manager, Alexandra also acts as Westminster Kingsway College's hospitality representative when the college hosts visitors from across the UK and beyond. She's the college's ambassador on overseas trips too, doing demonstrations and accompanying students to places such as China, Brazil, Finland and Cyprus.

Having been at Westminster Kingsway College for the best part of two decades, Alexandra has a strong connection with it. It has also played another rather more unexpected role in her life too: it's where she met her husband, chef lecturer Barry Jones.

"We've been together 14 years and we got married last year," she says. "I've been single all my life, had no intention of getting married or living with anybody. I'd got my life sorted here, career, flat in Canary Wharf – I was set. Then he went and changed the lot!"

Chef Team

The bulk of Westminster Kingsway College's teaching team is made up of chef lecturers – the members of staff whose job it is to hand down their knowledge in practical and theoretical lessons across the college's various courses. They're an incredibly diverse group of people, but no matter how different their backgrounds, they're all drawn from the very highest levels of the hospitality industry.

As national chairman of the Craft Guild of Chefs, **Chris Basten** is fairly close to the top of that industry. The Guild – derived from the Universal Cookery and Food Association, the organisation historically responsible for founding Westminster Kingsway College – works to promote good cookery and the hospitality industry as a whole. Since November 2012, Chris has juggled his role as chairman of this important group with a chef lecturer role at Westminster Kingsway College.

"I've just come in from the industry so I can show the students different ways of preparation techniques and plating up, because it's an industry that's fluid and moving all the time," he says. "And as I judge competitions all the time, I get to see different things that are happening, which is useful."

As well as judging competitions, Chris has taken part in many himself, with considerable success. He's also worked at the Ritz and Dorchester hotels, and completed apprenticeships with great chefs like Raymond Blanc and John Burton-Race – a considerable wealth of experience to share with Westminster Kingsway College's keen students.

Tony Cameron's past ventures are similarly impressive – Claridges, the Connaught, the Savoy and the Berkeley to name a few. Tony is also a member of the Craft Guild of Chefs, as well as the Master Chefs of Great Britain, and he's a fellow of the Royal Academy of Culinary Arts too. He's enjoying his latest role, as Westminster Kingsway College chef lecturer, just as much.

"It's nice to be able to pass something over to students, isn't it?" he says. "I'm teaching the students here exactly how I taught the guys who were working for me. It's no different except that there are more of them and it's a more controlled environment."

Tony has only been a member of the Westminster Kingsway College team for a short while, but he has already been bowled over by the standards on display.

"The teaching here is second to none," he says. "Some of the guys here are brilliant. I've got a lot of respect for them. They care about the students; they care about succeeding."

Success is something **Vince Cottam** knows plenty about. As a member of the Westminster Kingsway College Culinary Arts Competition Team, he's mentored students to success in many competitive events, including the 2012 Toque d'Or contest. He's also a past winner of the Craft Guild of Chefs Competition Chef Award. It's a part of his job that's proved incredibly rewarding.

Chris Basten

Vince Cottam

Tony Cameron

Norman Fu

Paul Jervis

Andrew Lansdell

Jose Souto

"To see that smile on their face that they've actually won something... even now I get parents ringing me up saying 'thank you for what you've done for my son or daughter,'" says Vince. "That's what I like, giving people a chance."

Vince spent 27 years as a chef in the Royal Navy, eventually working his way up to become the private chef of the chief of defence staff, a position which saw him cooking for prime ministers and the Prince of Wales amongst others. While thinking about a change of career in 2002, he was offered a chef lecturer role at Westminster Kingsway College, and since then he hasn't looked back.

"It's not really like a job, this – it's like a hobby, isn't it? You're coming in and doing something that you love, and you find something different every day," he says. "Some days the students walk out of my class laughing their heads off, but always learning. I've not had one person fall to sleep on me yet!"

For **Norman Fu**, the best thing about being a Westminster Kingsway College chef lecturer is helping with the student's development.

"It's nice to see the progression, when they come in from secondary school and they know very little, or they have the enthusiasm for the career but don't know how to go about it," he says. "They mature, emotionally, skill-wise, knowledge-wise, and it's very nice to see."

Norman trained as a chef in his father's restaurant, before a career change which saw him going to Hong Kong to teach English. When he returned to London, he was asked to fill a vacant spot in the chef lecturer team at Westminster Kingsway College. That was in 1999 and he has been here ever since.

For Norman, the college is a place worth going the extra mile for – for students as well as staff. "Last year, we had a student who travelled in from Somerset every week," he says. "He would come in on Sunday night, stay with his aunt in London and on Friday night he'd go back to Somerset. Every week for three years he did that!"

Like Vince, Norman is a member of the college's competition team. So too is **Jose Souto** – although his role is even more central to the competition process. Jose is the college's unofficial competition 'fixer'. He liaises with external PR companies and food producers, who provide products or ingredients for the students to cook with, as well as prizes for the winners. This is beneficial for both parties: students increase their skills and knowledge, while the companies get excellent press coverage and exposure. Past providers have included Alaska Seafood and Parmesan, amongst many, many others. Jose is also a judge and chair of a number of external competitions, including the Quality Food Awards and the Spanish Young Chef of the Year, and is a member of the Craft Guild of Chefs too. "The college and Gary have been good enough to just let me do my stuff," he says.

Jose is also a former Westminster Kingsway College

student. After leaving the college, he worked in Spain, before landing a job in the House of Commons. A keen falconer and deerstalker, Jose developed a knowledge of and passion for game during his time at the Commons. He produced a training manual on the subject and off the back of that was invited to deliver some lectures at his old college. It was this which saw him being offered the permanent position he has here today.

Jose's game expertise means that he spends most of his time teaching in the college's boucherie classes, as well as delivering external game seminars. His keen interest in food provenance also led him to set up the model of sustainability that the college adheres to today. Clearly, Jose's passion for this place runs deep, and he feels it's the college's overarching philosophy that sets it apart from the rest.

"There is this thing here called 'the Westminster Way', which is basically to stretch and challenge our students beyond the normal curriculum," he says. "We don't have to do that, but it's the way we've always taught, and Gary and the team expect this. The kids go out of here more employable, I think, than any other college."

Like Jose, **Paul Jervis** is another ex-Westminster Kingsway College student-turned-current-Westminster Kingsway College chef lecturer. After leaving the college in 1996, he pursued a career in contract catering, working his way up to head chef positions in the dining facilities of some of London's top companies. But he was always interested in teaching, and thanks to a wonderful coincidence, he was able to come back to his old college to do just that.

"I phoned up Simon Stocker and said 'I want to get into teaching at some stage. Give me some advice about what my next move should be,'" says Paul. "He said, 'we've got a job going now – the application closes tomorrow.' It was fate, it really was!"

Paul, who is course co-ordinator for the first year Professional Chef Diploma programme, believes the different experiences that Westminster Kingsway College's students are exposed to add a huge amount of value to their education here. "The internet is a wonderful resource but there's nothing that can compare to going to a market and picking up a variety of tomato, smelling it, tasting it, learning by experience," he says. "That's what gives them the depth of knowledge. Their passion for food is going to be much bigger."

Like Paul, **Andrew Lansdell** also came to Westminster Kingsway College from the contract catering business. He made the move into teaching on a recommendation from a former boss who had also joined the Westminster Kingsway College team and Andrew's glad he followed in his footsteps.

"It's very fulfilling," he says. "The hard bit is trying to mould the students. It's good to see them over the year learning and picking up new skills."

Andrew, who currently teaches on the first year Professional Chef Diploma programme, has maintained his links with the industry – something that helps his students no end when it comes to their externships, or work experience placements. "It gives them a very wide spectrum of what's out there for them when they leave – it gives them a taste of what they can do," he says. "Other colleges may not be as fortunate in terms of where we are and the links that we have, but that's done through a lot of people throughout the college working hard to establish those links. It wouldn't have happened without that."

Stefan Greubel is course co-ordinator for the second year Professional Chef Diploma programme, a role which mainly involves developing menus for The Vincent Room Brasserie and supervising student's work in the restaurant kitchen. "I've reached the stage in my life where I want to pass on my experience to the next generation," he says.

Originally from Munich, Stefan brings with him the extensive knowledge gained from a career that has taken him all over the world. He's worked in top-flight restaurants and hotels in places such as Belgium, France, Switzerland, Italy and Singapore, learning no fewer than five languages in the process, and is also a successful competition chef with a string of gold medals to his name. Seeking a change of pace from restaurant life and its 16-hour days, Stefan came to Westminster Kingsway College as a chef lecturer, and he's never looked back. "What I like best about this job is seeing somebody who can't cook an egg, watching them grow and then getting a very recognised and accepted position in the industry," he says.

Jonathon Warner, course co-ordinator for the Professional Chef Diploma third year, believes the college plays a vital role in inspiring students to take those respected industry positions. "What we want for our students is to aim as high as they can – we don't want them to take the easy route," he says. "It's very important that we stay linked to the best of the best, so that students can see what we expect of them."

Jonathon, who teaches mainly in the fine dining Escoffier restaurant, has an illustrious background of cooking in top hotels and restaurants. He's been at Westminster Kingsway College for almost five years now, working his way up to his current co-ordinator position. It's a role that helps him to shape student's experience for the good.

"I think it's just about developing year on year, trying to add value to the students in terms of learning and experiences," he says. "That means trying to make sure that everything about the course is valid and relevant and it pushes the students every year. We're always evaluating, trying to improve what we do."

For **Miranda Godfrey**, being a chef lecturer at Westminster Kingsway College is a dream job. "It's such a diverse place to work. You're meeting new people all the time. High profile people from industry are always working with us at the college," she says. "Raymond Blanc coming in was a bit of a wobbly leg moment!"

Miranda is course co-ordinator for the International Culinary Diploma, which sees her teaching students from across the globe. Before coming to Westminster Kingsway College, Miranda had a successful career as a chef, working in director's dining amongst other things. She's also enjoyed victory in many competitive cooking events, and enjoys passing on her skills in that field to her students. But the biggest thrill was just coming to Westminster Kingsway College in the first place.

"I really didn't think I would get the job because it was such a high-profile college, so I was over the moon when I got it," she says. "And I never thought teaching would be the thing... I was always a chef. But I do love what I do – giving something back."

That's a sentiment **Barry Jones** agrees with. "It's the opportunity of passing on the skills and knowledge that I've got to other people," he says. "I enjoy demonstrating and talking about breaking down a hind-quarter of beef, for example, because it's important that these particular skills are absorbed and learned by our students for their future in the industry. Not many colleges seem to cover butchery skills and the inherent knowledge of wastage, cost control and provenance."

As you may have guessed, one of Barry's specialisms here at Westminster Kingsway College is butchery – but that's only one string of his bow. He's the longest-serving member of the current teaching team, and at present teaches across a number of courses, including the Professional Chef Diploma delivery in the garde manger. While Barry has always been proud to be involved with Westminster Kingsway College, he feels right now it is the strongest it has ever been.

"Having been here for 25 years, I've seen how everything has progressed," says Barry, who was a chef in the army before moving into education. "We've had Gary lead us now for a few years. He's very forward-thinking, very focused, and that comes down the chain to us lecturers."

Like Barry, **Simon Stocker** is another long-standing member of the Westminster Kingsway College team, and he too recognises the quality of the college's lecturers. "The staff here work very hard," he says. "They're not like normal lecturers at other colleges, but we're not a normal school."

Simon has worked in many different capacities in the college, and has made his mark on the culinary arts and hospitality department in a myriad of ways over the years, including helping to develop the current format of the Escoffier menu. His role now is Advanced Practitioner in Culinary Arts, a senior position which sees him supporting the lecturers in their teaching, and monitoring assessments

Jonathon Warner

Stefan Greubel

Simon Stocker

Miranda Godfrey

Barry Jones

Volta Bushay

John King

Allan Drummond

Dr Rachel Edwards-Stuart

Claire Rankin

Duties Of Head Chef

and standards. He still spends time with the students, though, both as a lecturer and a competition mentor, in which capacity he's had significant success, at events such as the World Culinary Olympics amongst others.

Simon – a former Westminster Kingsway College student, having studied here part-time whilst working in top London restaurants, clubs and casinos – feels that it's important for the college to help its students to be able to stand on their own two feet in the hospitality industry. "That's what we should be doing here. It's not just about teaching them how to cook and be an automated robot, it's about them thinking for themselves," he says.

"I don't care if they're not going to be the best chef in the world, as long as they're going to be a chef who wants to improve all the time. Whenever I interview students I say the same thing: 'you never stop learning in this job. You can't know it all – you can only have an appreciation of things.'"

In a roundabout way, **Volta Bushay** has been here almost as long as Barry Jones. She came to the college in the late 1980s as a kitchen technician and has progressed up the ranks to her current position as chef lecturer. But as she explains, teaching wasn't always part of the plan.

"I started off with the intention of being a chef in top hotel restaurants," says Volta. "I worked at a Hilton hotel for a while, then I went to the University of London as a deputy catering manageress, so that's where the education started for me."

Volta went on to work for Nacro, the crime reduction charity that helps to rehabilitate young offenders, before coming to Westminster Kingsway College. Now a mainstay of the college's chef team, she's known to the students as 'Aunty Volta'.

"I enjoy teaching students," she says. "I'm from a very large family where there are a lot of young people, and I've always been able to guide them and offer advice. This job is not just about teaching them, because quite often I find myself offering a shoulder of, support when they need it. There are always students who want advice and you have to be prepared to steer them in the right direction."

Volta may not have intended to become a lecturer but it's a role she enjoys and excels at. It's a similar story with **Allan Drummond**. His love for cooking started at a young age, but his career unfolded in a rather unexpected way.

"I come from a big family, so I used to watch my mum produce food from virtually nothing to feed us all, and that always used to fascinate me," he says. "I came down to London in 1970 for six months, and it has been a long six months as I'm still here!"

For many years, Allan worked at four- and five-star hotels and restaurants in his native Scotland and then London, cooking for royalty, presidents and rock stars along the way. After being asked to lecture at a college, he got the teaching

time basis. After taking a year out to travel the world with his wife, he joined the team full-time in 2005.

Allan loves being able to pass on the skills he's picked up over a long career to a new generation of young chefs. He believes he's at the best place in the world to do that – something that was confirmed for him on his round-the-world adventure...

"I was in a little hotel in Nevada, in the middle of nowhere – five bedrooms in it, five couples staying," he says. "The lounge was where everybody came and sat – there was no other place to go. We were all talking, and there was a girl there who was the bass guitarist for the rock band My Bloody Valentine. She said to me 'what do you do for work?' And I said 'I'm a chef lecturer at Westminster Kingsway College'. She said 'you're joking – every time I'm in London, I take my mum to the Vincent Rooms for lunch!'

"And there was an American there, an archaeologist – he said every time he's in London he eats in the Escoffier. He was talking about the duck press on the window! I knew how popular Westminster Kingsway College was, but it wasn't until I travelled that I realised just how far the name goes."

The chef team is completed by chef lecturers **Gopalene Mootien**, **John King** and **Claire Rankin**. There is one more member, however – someone with a slightly different role to the rest. **Dr Rachel Edwards-Stuart** is the college's culinary science lecturer. Working from Westminster Kingsway College's newly-installed culinary science laboratory – the only facility of its type in any further education institution in the world – she teaches students the science behind food, as well as the innovative concepts of modernist, experimental cuisine. Rachel also undertakes academic research in this field of study. But how did she arrive at the college?

"I did my undergraduate degree in biochemistry, so not food science at all, but was always passionate about food," she says.

"I got the opportunity to go and work for Herve This in Paris, who's one of the fore-founders of molecular gastronomy. I worked with him in his research lab, on the science of potato salad. I then moved back to the UK to do a PhD that was sponsored by Heston Blumenthal. I worked for him for three years exploring how you could actually use a full-on science laboratory and scientific research team to create something slightly more complex, more challenging ideas."

Around this time Rachel began delivering lectures to chefs about culinary science, and it was off the back of this that she was invited to Westminster Kingsway College. Despite both the college's culinary science programme and Rachel's teaching career being in their infancy, she's already looking to the future.

"As time goes on we'll continue to develop and improve the courses," she says. It is a very exciting time at

Pastry Team

Westminster Kingsway College's chef team is supplemented by a group of lecturers specialising in pastry. Gary Hunter is just one of the many people keen to sing their praises.

"This is the best pastry team I've ever seen at Westminster Kingsway College, and I've been here a while now," he says. "We've always had a strong pastry team here, but this is the biggest specialist pastry teaching team in the UK and arguably the most skilful in terms of their experience, their knowledge and their commitment to teaching. It's testament to them that this academic year we have seen record numbers of students wanting to go through to do third-year pastry. They are so articulate and so engaging in what they do that they really inspire talent and passion in students. I can't speak highly enough."

There's no question that Westminster Kingsway College's

Yolande Stanley. After a career as head pastry chef in some of London's most exclusive establishments, including the Ritz and Landmark hotels, she moved into teaching, coming to Westminster Kingsway College on a part-time basis around three years ago.

Yolande is also the UK training manager for patisserie and confectionery with WorldSkills, the prestigious international training competition, and is one of only four people in the country to date to have been awarded the title of Master of Culinary Arts in Pastry from the Royal Academy of Culinary Arts.

Yolande's staggering CV and close connections to the industry, not to mention her passion for teaching, mean she's perfectly placed to teach Westminster Kingsway College's keen pastry students. "I'm at the cutting edge of the technology, ideas and current trends all the time, which

Yolande Stanley

Jessica Courtis

Ashley Spencer

kind of addicted to learning. I take myself off on courses and whatever else I can think of doing, just constantly updating my skills base."

Yolande brings the benefit of years of experience to her role as pastry chef lecturer at Westminster Kingsway College. **Jessica Courtis** may not have as many years under her belt just yet, but her natural flair for teaching is just as strong. Before joining the pastry team here, she was at The Bertinet Kitchen, the cookery school of French baker and author Richard Bertinet. It was Jessica's skilled work here that brought her into contact with Westminster Kingsway College.

"Westminster Kingsway College lecturers came to the Bertinet School, because they'd heard about Richard and they wanted to implement his method of bread-making into the college," she says. "They saw how I was teaching and offered me the job! This has given me a great opportunity to

teach important bakery skills to all of our many students using some fantastic organic UK flours."

At Westminster Kingsway College, Jessica heads up the new bakery, which is also taught by **Ashley Spencer**. A proud Aussie, he trained in his next door neighbour's bakery, before working in top hotels across Australia. In 1998, he went travelling around Asia and Europe, eventually ending up in the UK but the reason he's still here is purely by chance...

"I walked into an internet café and they said 'are you here about the bar job?', and I said, 'yeah, alright!'" From this moment of opportunism, Ashley worked his way up through various roles, from front of house to kitchen, eventually securing an executive chef job at a Hilton hotel. This role involved staff training, and when Ashley's skill at this was mentioned to him, he moved into teaching, joining the Westminster Kingsway College team in 2006.

Ashley is also course co-ordinator for the college's part-time programmes, his time split between teaching professional cookery and in the college's bakery – a large and demanding operation. "We have three sections in the bakery: the dough section, the lamination section and the afternoon tea pastry section," he says. "With the dough section we get in at seven in the morning to start producing all the doughs for the bread that we're going to be using for both the restaurants, for selling in the shop, for the canteen and so on."

The pastry teaching operation at Westminster Kingsway College, both in the bakery and in other areas of the college, is huge, which makes having experienced pastry chef lecturers all the more important.

In pastry chef lecturer **Jacqui Holland**, the team has just that.

"My last job was at the British Airways head office. We did lots of fine dining for the first class lounges at Heathrow – I was the head pastry chef there," she says. "I've had about 20 years in industry. I've been here at the college about four years. It was part time groups and other bits and pieces when I first came, and with my experience I've progressed onto more specialised patisserie programmes."

Jacqui is an old college classmate of Yolande's, and one of the things she loves most about teaching here is that the pair – and indeed the entire pastry team – sing from the same song sheet. "We've had similar training, with the late Professor John Huber," she says. "It's great to bounce ideas off each other. We've got certain standards and it's important to us that our students understand this."

Huber was a renowned pastry chef and trainer, and in addition to Jacqui and Yolande, he was also the mentor to another member of the Westminster Kingsway College pastry team – **Sue Yeates**. As she says, his training has set the team here in excellent stead.

"Some things you look at now and you're thinking 'that seems like ages ago – I don't remember doing that,'" she says.

Sue Yeates

Andy Whitson

Huber?' He's quite often a reference we go back to."

Sue is relatively new to the team, having joined in 2012. She came straight from a career in the industry, which included work in the contract catering field and five-star hotels such as the Mayfair. In a short time, she's proven herself an integral member of the teaching staff, despite her initial reluctance.

"People used to say to me 'you should go into teaching,'" she says. "I'd say 'no, they won't listen to me, they'll all be taller than me!'" Despite this, Sue is now responsible for the Pastry Kitchen, as well as teaching all of the desserts for both restaurants and the college canteen for the Professional Chef Diploma.

Completing the pastry team are **Steve Moss**, **Ian Sutton** and **Andy Whitson**. Andy's long career has taken many twists and turns but always revolving around two constants: cookery and teaching. After training as a chef, he worked in restaurants in Germany and the UK, moving up the kitchen brigade to become head chef. After owning and running his own restaurant for a spell, he went to work as a chef trainer for the Ministry of Defence, then on to college training roles.

In 2006, he and his family packed up and moved to Normandy, where he opened his own cookery school business, Oui Chef. Three years ago, he joined the Westminster Kingsway College team and he now commutes to the college from his home in France. That's some serious dedication – but as Andy himself says, this is a place that's more than worth the effort.

"I don't think I'd do it for any other college really," he says. "I love it. The work here is great, it's a nice team, you're in London and this is the 100-year-old school founded by Escoffier! It's amazing to be here." Andy has taken charge of the college's new International Patisserie Diploma course, which is so popular the college are planning to run more classes in the new academic year.

Jacqui Holland

Ian Sutton

Food & Beverage Service & Hospitality Team

As its name suggests, Westminster Kingsway College's School of Hospitality and Culinary Arts covers both sides of the industry. As well as the college's skilled chef lecturers teaching cookery training, there are also some equally talented staff teaching the hospitality side of things as well.

Zoe Adjey is one of Westminster Kingsway College's food and beverage and hospitality lecturers. She's also a published author of Food and Beverage Service by Cengage. Originally from Northern Ireland, she brings a wealth of experience to her role at the college.

"I came and studied hospitality management here in London and then worked in restaurants in the West End," she says. "I eventually became trainee manager and HR manager for the company that ran The Ivy. I spent seven years there doing most of their training. I always said that the only job I would ever leave The Ivy for would be a job in education, and the only job I'd ever leave for in education would be in vocational education, because I know from when I was in industry that's where the bit of recruiting didn't work."

Zoe is also course co-ordinator for the college's Diploma in Hospitality Management, a role which allows her to fulfil that ambition of helping to train the students who will hopefully fill that gap in the hospitality industry. It's a role she truly adores.

"I love it – it's the best job in the world," she says. "You can guarantee that no two days will be the same. I'm still at the heart of the industry, still doing something incredibly worthwhile."

Veronique Bonnefoy came to Westminster Kingsway College from Gordon Ramsay Holdings, where she was training manager for the chef's group of Michelin starred restaurants. It was a role that prepared her perfectly for working as a lecturer at the college. "It was a fabulous job that gave me a big foot in here, because I knew what I was talking about with the experience gained from such an important industry leader," she says.

Veronique has been at the college since 2005. Her current role is that of restaurant service and wine education course leader. She specialises in teaching front of house service and also delivers modules on wine matching and managing the cellar. Like Zoe, she too gets great pleasure from her work here.

"I think it's a little bit like an artist – you know you've got a skill for getting on with people, passing on the message and wanting to see them improve," she says. "I just love to see the effect it has on the kids. They come, they think they're rubbish and within a week they look at you and they think 'I can do that.' That's a superb reward."

Westminster Kingsway College's food and beverage service and hospitality team is completed by food and beverage lecturer **Simon Willson-White**, **Lindsey Lamont** and **Richard Dixon.**

Zoe Adjey

Lindsey Lamont

Richard Dixon

Simon Willson-White

Veronique Bonnefoy

Rose Gibson (second left)

And...

The staff here at Westminster Kingsway are a mixture of those new to the college and those who have been here for many years. But there's one lady whose tenure at Vincent Square is longer than all of them. She isn't a lecturer, though – she's canteen supervisor **Rose Gibson**.

Rose came to Westminster Kingsway College in 1980 – on 10th May, to be precise. She's witnessed many changes in the college over the years, but her love for this historic place has never wavered, even in tougher times.

"Over the years it was extremely hard work – we didn't have all the mod cons that you'd have today," she says. "We were 'The Bucket Ladies' – everything used to go in buckets!"

Local girl Rose (she lives within walking distance) is

Westminster Kingsway College. Her mother May Bolster was here for around 20 years starting from 1974. May remembers one of the college's most famous sons, Jamie Oliver – although you might not necessarily describe those memories as fond ones...

"When he was here, my mum used to chase him along the corridor," says Rose. "He was a cheeky chap!"

After more than three decades here, retirement may be on the horizon for Rose. When she does decide to leave Westminster Kingsway College, however, she has plenty to reminisce about.

"The cakes used to be a penny, a cup of tea used to be threepence," she says. "We didn't even have a till in those

The Restaurants

The Vincent Rooms are the beating (heating, stirring, pouring) heart of Westminster Kingsway College. It's here in the college's two restaurants – the Brasserie and the Escoffier – that students really get to put the skills and knowledge they've gained in lessons to the test. As the restaurants are open to the public, they're doing so for paying customers too.

For the majority of students, a shift at The Vincent Rooms is their first experience of working a busy restaurant service. Dishes must be prepared not only to the exacting standards of their lecturer but on time and to order as well,

in a kitchen that's not just a realistic working environment but a real one. There's front-of-house to be taken care of too – tables to be waited on, diners to be greeted, burgeoning sommelier skills to be put into practical use.

The Brasserie is the larger of the two restaurants; a bright, airy room at the front of the college building with space for up to 160 guests. The smaller Escoffier is Westminster Kingsway College's fine dining restaurant, named after the college's famous founder. White linen, formal service and modern haute cuisine are the order of the day, with only third year students permitted to cook here.

Lecturers take charge of the restaurants with the students entering on a rotational basis, acting as head chef with the students as their brigade. Menus are devised by the lecturer, and they change regularly according to seasonality and the availability of ingredients, the same as in any restaurant worth its salt (or, indeed, pepper).

The Brasserie menu changes on a daily basis to reflect the availability and the provenance of commodities, whereas the menu in the Escoffier changes weekly, with the final year chef students working hard to hone classic dishes and contemporary ideas and presentations which Auguste

Escoffier himself would approve of. The Vincent Rooms have had their fair share of praise over the years, and in this chapter you'll find some of the reviews and accolades the restaurants have received. Also presented is a selection of classic dishes served at Westminster Kingsway College throughout its history, from those created by Escoffier himself to the contemporary cuisine produced at the college today.

Famous staff and students may be Westminster Kingsway College's enduring legacy, but the food and service at The Vincent Rooms remains its beating heart.

Toby Young
Evening Standard, 16 June 2006

Since it's part of an educational establishment, The Vincent Rooms is not intended to be profitable and, perhaps for that reason, the prices are absurdly reasonable. For instance, a starter of linguine with basil, garlic, salami and olives is £3.50, while the most expensive main course – roasted duck breast with potato Cretan and green beans – is only £9.50. In effect, you can have a decent two-course meal for the price of a sandwich and a cup of coffee at Starbucks.

I started with smoked chicken Caesar salad and followed up with veal cordon bleu. Both dishes were exemplary. Whoever prepared my salad had gone to the trouble of rolling the anchovies into little worm-like shapes – a nice touch, I thought – and the veal escalope was even better than my wife's.

I get letters from readers every week claiming that such-and-such a place is an 'undiscovered gem' – usually an Indian or a Greek that just happens to be five minutes' walk from their house. Nine times out of ten, these places turn out to be perfectly decent neighbourhood restaurants, but nothing special.

The Vincent Rooms, by contrast, is the real McCoy. If it's value for money you're after, I don't think you'll find a better deal in London. Once word gets out, your only problem will be booking a table.

Matthew Norman
The Guardian, 21 November 2009

This is a highly impressive restaurant in its own right. For one thing, the large, square space is very handsome, with its floor-to-ceiling windows, polished floorboards, elegant hanging lamps and Regency panelling.

My friend went for osso bucco, risotto Milanese and gremolata with a rocket, pine nut and parmesan salad. The veal shank – like all the meat, butchered on the premises – was "excellent... There's probably a bit too much going on here, but you could do much worse in a fancy West End place." My roasted breast of guinea fowl with all the trimmings – liver croute, bread sauce, game chips et al – would have graced a Michelin joint, the meat being crispy-skinned and juicy, and cleverly complemented by a lively whisky jus.

A rich chocolate pudding with clotted cream and "impeccable" bakewell tart were outstanding, and as a chap who appeared to be 14 wandered through the room in his chef's garb, the beams of avuncular pleasure became even more immovably fixed. An implausibly miniscule bill stretched them even farther until the facial muscles screamed for mercy, and we left utterly charmed by a venture that combines the indulgence of youth with professional rigour far, far better than this review.

The Independent 100 Best Restaurants in the UK, 16 June 2007

Westminster Kingsway College has turned out such illustrious chefs as Ainsley Harriott and Jamie Oliver – and you can eat very good food at a very good price in the college restaurant.

Artisan bread from our bakery,

and a classic ingredient prepared the Westminster Kingsway way

Five Seed Bread

Makes 4 x 400g pieces

Ingredients:

Soaked Overnight (soaker)
200g Five seed flour
250g Water

Ferment
250g Malt flour
200g Water
1g Yeast
5g Salt

Dough
500g Strong white flour
200g Water
17g Salt
12g Yeast
+ Soaked seeds
+ Ferment

You will also need:
Linen cloths
Extra 5 seed flour for topping the loaves with.

Method:

1. Make the soaker and the ferment 14 hours before using. Mix the seeds with the water for the soaker, which will soften the seeds.

2. For the ferment rub the yeast in to the flour and add the salt and water, mix together with a whisk until combined and leave in a container or bowl covered over.

3. Preheat the oven to 250°C with two upturned oven trays ready to place the dough straight on to.

4. For the dough rub the yeast in to the flour, add the salt and mix. Add the soaker and the ferment to the flour. Pour in the water and mix together with a dough scraper. Take your time to mix as it will take a while to get everything incorporated together.

5. Turn the dough out on to the work surface; do not put flour down first. Use your dough scraper to gather the dough together and scrape into a ball. Using both hands, pick up the dough and work it to aerate the dough and to stretch the gluten. Each time pick up the dough and fold it down onto the table, this will trap air inside the dough making it lighter in texture.

6. Keep doing this working process for about five minutes, stopping to scrape in between to keep the dough together, which will help the dough to become less sticky.

7. Once the dough is formed, dust with a small amount of flour on the surface of the dough and inside the bowl. Cover with a linen cloth and leave to rest for 1-2 hours.

8. Once the dough has doubled in size, turn the dough out and divide into 400g pieces.

9. To mould the dough into loaves turn the smooth side down and press the dough out with the heel of your hand. Fold over one half of the dough into the centre and press down. Then fold the other half over and seal. Keep folding each side over and reinforcing the centre until the piece feels tighter and well moulded. Take the piece of dough and brush the top surface with water, place some of the seeds in a wide bowl and dip each loaf into the seeds so that they stick to the surface.

10. Prove each of the pieces on linen cloth, folded up so that each piece of dough has some cloth to stop them from sticking to each other. Or in a loaf tin which has been greased first. Leave to prove for 30-45 minutes.

11. When ready to bake, use semolina on oven trays or peels, to load into the oven to help the dough to slide off easily. Use a lame or very sharp knife first to make a score down the top of the loaf to create a burst. If using loaf tins you can still score the top of each loaf before placing the tins straight into the oven.

12. Steam-spray the oven sides and transfer the dough into the oven. When all the dough is in the oven, spray the oven sides and the door whilst closing to trap in as much steam as possible. This will create a good atmosphere for the dough which will help to create the bursts and develop a good crust. Bake well for about 15 minutes at 250°C then turn the temperature down to 220°C for a further 15-20 minutes.

13. Take the bread out of the tins to cool on a wire rack. Leave to cool completely before cutting into the bread.

Rye and Guinness Bread

Makes 4 x 420g loaves

Ingredients:

800g Strong white flour

200g Dark rye flour

20g Fresh yeast

20g Salt

400g Water

250g Guinness

25g Molasses

1 tsp Liquid malt extract

1 tsp Caraway seeds

Method:

1. Preheat the oven to 250°C, with two upturned oven trays ready to place the dough straight onto.

2. Rub the yeast into the flour. Add the salt and blend the dry ingredients together, with the caraway seeds. Mix the Guinness with the water, malt extract and the molasses. Pour all of the liquid in and mix with a dough scraper until you have a 'sticky' mixture and all is combined well.

3. Turn the dough out onto the work surface; do not sprinkle flour on the work surface first. Use your dough scraper to gather the dough together and scrape into a ball. Using both hands, pick up the dough and work it to aerate the dough and to stretch the gluten. Each time pick up the dough and fold it down onto the table, this will trap air inside the dough making it lighter in texture.

4. Keep doing this working process for about five minutes, stopping to scrape in between to keep the dough together, which will help the dough to become less sticky.

5. Once the dough is formed, dust with a small amount of rye flour on the surface of the dough and inside the bowl. Cover with a linen cloth and leave to rest for 1-2 hours.

6. Once the dough has doubled in size, turn the dough out and divide into 4 equal pieces (420g). Weighing is more accurate.

7. Now mould each piece of dough into a cob shaped loaf. Turn the smooth side down and press the dough out with the heel of your hand. Fold over one half of the dough in to the centre and press down. Then fold the other half over and seal. Keep folding each side over and reinforcing the centre until the piece feels tighter and well moulded. Place them into long linen lined baskets with the seam side up so that the baskets help to keep the shape of the dough.

8. Prove these now until the dough has relaxed, in a draught free area covered with a linen cloth. This should take between 30-45 minutes in a warm place. Leave for longer if the dough still feels tight.

9. Place semolina onto bread boards or an oven tray to help you to transfer the dough to the oven. Turn the dough out, seam side down, and smooth off the excess flour. Using a lame or a very sharp knife cut the surface of the dough with 3 diagonal slits across the top of the loaf. This action needs to be quick but also quite deep to make sure that the dough when baking will burst open in the correct way.

10. Steam-spray the oven sides and transfer the dough into the oven. Once the four pieces are in the oven, spray again and onto the oven door whilst closing it. This will create a good moist atmosphere for the dough which will help to create the bursts and develop a good crust.

11. Bake well for about 15 minutes at 250°C then turn the temperature down to 220°C for a further 15-20 minutes.

12. Leave to cool completely before cutting into the bread.

White Bread
Makes 3 Round Loaves

Ingredients:
1kg Strong white flour
20g Maldon sea salt
25g Fresh yeast
700ml Water
Semolina for dusting

Equipment:
3 x Linen lined round baskets
1 x Linen cloth

Method:
1. Preheat the oven to 250°C, with two upturned oven trays ready to place the dough straight onto.
2. Rub the yeast into the flour. Add the salt and blend the dry ingredients together. Pour all of the water in and mix with a dough scraper until you have a 'sticky' mixture and all of the flour and water is combined.
3. Turn the dough out onto the work surface; do not put flour down first. Use your scraper to gather the dough together and scrape into a ball. Using both hands, pick it up and work to aerate and to stretch the gluten. Each time pick up the dough and fold it down onto the table, this will trap air inside making it lighter in texture.
4. Keep doing this working process for about 5 minutes, stopping to scrape in between to keep the dough together, which will help it become less sticky.
5. Once the dough is formed, dust with a small amount of flour on the surface and inside the bowl. Cover with a linen cloth and leave to rest for 1-2 hours.
6. When the dough has doubled in size, turn it out and divide into 3 equal pieces (580g). Weighing is more accurate. Now mould each piece in to a round shape, by tucking all of the edges into the centre to create a tight ball. Place each round in to small linen lined bread baskets, with the seam side facing up.
7. Prove these now until the dough has relaxed, in a draught free area covered with a linen cloth. This should take between 30-45 minutes in a warm place. Leave for longer if it still feels tight.
8. Place the semolina onto bread boards or an oven tray to help you to transfer the dough to the oven. Turn it out seam side down and smooth off the excess flour. Using a lame, or a very sharp knife, cut the surface of the dough in the letters W, K, C. This action needs to be quick but also quite deep to make sure that the dough will burst in the right way when baking for the letters to show.
9. Steam-spray the oven sides and transfer the dough in to the oven. Once the 3 pieces are in the oven, spray again and on the oven door whilst closing it. This will create a good atmosphere and will help to create the bursts and develop a good crust. Bake well for about 15 minutes at 250°C then turn the temperature down to 220°C for a further 15-20 minutes.
10. Leave to cool on a wire rack completely before cutting into the bread.

Wholemeal Bread with Rum Soaked Prunes

Ingredients:

600g Wholemeal flour

400g Strong white flour

20g Fine sea salt

25g Fresh yeast

710ml Water

250g Prunes d'agen

100ml Dark rum

Method:

1. Leave the prunes to soak in the rum for at least a day as they will absorb the flavour and soften.

2. Preheat the oven to 250°C, with 2 upturned oven trays ready to place the dough straight onto.

3. Rub the yeast into the flour. Add the salt and blend the dry ingredients together. Pour all of the water in and mix with a dough scraper until you have a 'sticky' mixture and all of the flour and water is combined.

4. Turn the dough out onto the work surface; do not put flour down first. Use your scraper to gather the dough together and scrape into a ball. Using both hands, pick it up and work to aerate and to stretch the gluten. Each time pick up the dough and fold it down onto the table, this will trap air inside making it lighter in texture.

5. Keep doing this working process for about 5 minutes, stopping to scrape in between to keep the dough together, which will help it to become less sticky.

6. Once the dough is formed, turn it over so that the smooth side is facing down and open out to then put the rum soaked prunes in. Push the prunes into the dough and then fold tover to incorporate all of the mixture. Gently work as before to fold in the prunes and to create a smoother top surface.

7. Leave to rest in the bowl with a light dust of wholemeal flour for an hour. Divide the dough into 350g pieces and mould into oblong shapes. Do this by turning the smooth side down and pressing out. Fold over one half of the dough in to the centre and press down. Then fold the other half over and seal. Keep folding each side over and reinforcing the centre until the piece feels tighter and well moulded.

8. Prove each of the pieces on linen cloth, folded up so that each piece of dough has some cloth to stop them from sticking to each other. Leave to prove for 30-45 minutes.

9. When ready to bake, use semolina on oven trays or peels, to load into the oven, to help the dough to slide off easily. Use a lame or very sharp knife first to make a score down the top of the loaf to create a burst.

10. Steam-spray the oven sides and transfer the dough into the oven. Once the 3 pieces are in the oven, spray again and onto the oven door whilst closing it. This will create a good moist atmosphere for the dough which will help to create the bursts and develop a good crust.

11. Bake well for about 15 minutes at 250°C then turn the temperature down to 220°C for a further 15-20 minutes.

12. Leave to cool completely before cutting into the bread.

Smoked Salmon 'Westminster'

Makes one whole side of salmon

Ingredients:

1 Whole fresh salmon

500g Table salt

500g Granulated sugar

2 Oak wood briquettes

Method:

1. Take a whole side of salmon, leaving gill bone attached. Trim off any excess fat and remove the pin bones.

2. Mix the salt and sugar in a clean bowl thoroughly.

3. Place the side of salmon onto a large tray and cover with the salt and sugar curing mix.

4. Place into a refrigerator, uncovered for 24 hours. This allows the salt and sugar to cure the fish.

5. After 24 hours, remove the salmon from the refrigerator and wash off all the salt and sugar with clean cold water.

6. Dry the salmon well and place onto a dry tray and then place in the refrigerator again for 12 hours or overnight to allow drying.

7. Switch on cold smoker with the oak wood briquettes and allow 10 minutes for the smoke to build up inside the chamber of the Bradley Cold Smoker. Hang the salmon side up by gill bone using a hook and place into the smoker.

8. Allow the smoking process to run for at least 1 hour or longer if you would prefer a stronger smoke flavour to impart into the salmon.

9. Remove the salmon from smoker and seal in vacuum bags for storage in a refrigerator, or present ready for slicing and serving at the table.

Salad of Seasonal Game Bird with Seeds and Nuts, Bitter Leaf
Salad, Berries and a Berry Essence. See the recipe on page 85

The Brasserie

Cocktails

Beetroot Bellini

Our Restaurant Service team of teachers and students are always experimenting with ways to create the best and most unusual Bellini cocktail. This is one of our most popular Bellinis which we sometimes serve in our Brasserie Restaurant.

Ingredients:

Fresh beetroot

Prosecco

Method:

1. Carefully wash, peel and steam the beetroot and leave to cool down for a few minutes.

2. Blend the cooked beetroot to a purée and place this into a centrifuge set at 4000rpm for 30 minutes.

3. Drain off the liquid beetroot and place this into a pan with a medium heat applied. Bring the liquid to the boil and reduce until a caramel has formed from the natural sugars in the beetroot.

4. 15-20ml of the finished caramel is required for one glass of Bellini, topped up with Prosecco.

5. To create a garnish; this is a thin slice of candied beetroot sitting on the rim of the Champagne flute. To make the candied beetroot, slice a raw beetroot thinly and dip in standard stock syrup (50% sugar/50% water). Wrap clingfilm tightly around a concave tray, place the sliced beetroot on top and set in a warm and dry oven chamber or dehydrator.

Bramble Cocktail

This is one of the best and most popular drinks to originate from the 1980s – created in the mid-80s by Dick Bradsell at Fred's Club, Soho, London, England. We have placed our own perspective on it by freezing the bramble in a spherical ball. It will chill the drink and as it melts it will change the colour of the drink. This element adds a little theatre to the drink in our Brasserie Restaurant as a pre-dinner aperitif.

Ingredients:

2 Shots Bombay London dry gin

1 Shot freshly squeezed lemon juice

½ Shot Monin pure cane sugar syrup

½ Shot Crème de Mûre liqueur

200g Fresh blackberries

Method:

1. Take the fresh blackberries and liquidise until smooth.

2. Put blackberry juice in a centrifuge and set to spin at 4000rpm for 30 minutes. Pour off the liquid blackberry layer and add the Crème de Mûre liqueur to this.

3. Place this liquid in spherical ice moulds to freeze.

4. Use an old fashioned style of cocktail glass to present this cocktail.

5. Place the frozen blackberry ice sphere in the base of the glass. Shake the London Gin, lemon juice and cane sugar syrup with ice and strain into the glass and over the ice sphere.

6. Serve with short straws. As the blackberry ice sphere melts, the bramble effect is seen.

7. Garnish with 2 blackberries.

Terrine of Foie Gras and Pheasant
Makes one terrine

First Stage – Ingredients:

775g Foie gras escalopes
200g Curing salt
200g Caster sugar
50g Crushed black pepper, roasted and cooled

Method:

1. Mix the curing salt, sugar and pepper together.
2. Sprinkle a layer on the bottom of a clean tray.
3. Place on the frozen foie gras escalopes and cover with the remaining salt/sugar/pepper mix.
4. Cover and allow to defrost completely, or for 4 hours. This will cure the foie gras to the correct degree. Place in a refrigerator.
5. Wash off the cure with cold running water, and using fish tweezers, remove any veins by grasping around the exposed vein and carefully pulling until it comes out. Repeat this process with all the escalopes, and then chill in a refrigerator until the escalopes have firmed.

Second stage:

Prepared foie gras from the first stage
100ml Sauternes
Vacuum bags
4 Pheasant breasts – de-boned
Curing salt
Hazelnut oil
200ml Chicken glace stock
Maldon salt and ground white pepper
1 x 1kg terrine mould, oiled and lined with clingfilm

Method:

1. Season the pheasant breasts with the curing salt. Place the pheasant breasts in a vacuum bag with some hazelnut oil and seal on a vacuum machine.
2. Place the foie gras escalopes (grouped in 6 per bag) into vacuum bags with some sauternes and seal on the highest setting (normally 1) on the vacuum machine and place back into the refrigerator until ready to cook sous vide.
3. Set a sous vide machine to 55°C, carefully place foie gras to cook for 30 minutes. Also cook the pheasant breasts for 30 minutes in the water bath at the same temperature.
4. Cut the bags and tip out onto a tray, trim the foie gras and pheasant breasts neatly to form rectangular slabs. Save the trim to use as filler for any gaps. Layer the foie gras with the pheasant breast meat in the terrine moulds, ensuring that the chicken glace is used as binding between the layers to hold everything together. Season well between each layer.
5. The final layer should be of foie gras. Press firmly down to expel any air pockets.
6. Make a cartouche of cardboard wrapped in foil and then clingfilm, ensuring that this fits the top of the terrine precisely.
7. Use a second terrine mould or weights to weigh down the terrine and place in the refrigerator for 12 hours minimum.
8. Once set, pull the terrine from its mould using the clingfilm you lined it with, re-wrap with at least 3 layers of clingfilm and place back into the refrigerator for service.

For service (4 portions):

4 Slices terrine (approximately 60g per portion)

4 Quenelles apricot and almond chutney (see seperate recipe below)

8 Caper berries, split in half

12 Chicken Madeira jelly cubes

40g Baby watercress

30g Parsley, chopped

Method:

1. Cut a slice of the terrine and roll the edges in the chopped parsley.

2. Place a slice of terrine in the middle of a plate.

3. Place a quenelle of chutney on the side. Place the chicken Madeira cubes on the side of the plate.

4. Arrange the caper berries on the plate.

5. Dress the baby watercress with a touch of the oil, and place on and around the terrine.

Apricot and Almond Chutney

Ingredients:

500g Semi-dried apricots, chopped small

500g Glace apricots, chopped small

500g Apricot purée

500g Sugar

1 litre White wine vinegar

250g Shallots, finely chopped

250g Nibbed almonds, roasted

Maldon salt

Method:

1. Caramelise the sugar in a dry clean saucepan.

2. Add the apricot purée and dissolve in the caramel. Carefully mix together.

3. Add the white wine vinegar, shallots and both types of apricots. Cook slowly to a chutney consistency, stirring every now and again.

4. Check the seasoning and consistency before cooling and finally adding the almonds.

5. Pour into pre-sterilised Kilner jars to set.

Clam Chowder

Salad of Seasonal Game Bird with Seeds and Nuts, Bitter Leaf Salad, Berries and a Berry Essence

4 portions

Ingredients:

4 breasts from small game bird (wood pigeon, mallard, teal, partridge or grouse) vacuum packed in olive oil and cooked using the sous vide method at 50°C for 20 minutes

25g Hazelnuts fried in butter

25g Sunflower seeds, toasted

25g Rolled oats, fried in butter

25g Caramelised pecans or walnuts

100g Bitter leaves washed and picked (chicory/baby rocket/radicchio)

50g Halved or torn berries (elder/blue/rasp/black)

Berry essence – this is naturally evaporated berry vinegar

Vinaigrette

Green oil

Maldon Salt and ground white pepper

Method:

1. Remove the game birds from the sous vide pouch, drain, season well, crisp the skin in oil in a hot pan, flip over and then remove to drain and rest in a warm place for a few minutes.
2. Mix together the oats, hazelnuts and sunflower seeds. Position the nuts onto four plates. Make a short line down the centre of the plate or to one side.
3. Scatter the berries around the plate.
4. Dress the leaves with vinaigrette and arrange on the seed mix.
5. Slice the game bird breasts and arrange over the salad.
6. Drizzle over and around, with the berry essence.
7. Apply the green oil decoratively around the plate.

See picture on page 78

Clam Chowder

2 portions

Ingredients:

200g Pallourde Clams

40g Pancetta

20g Leek, finely diced

20g Onion, finely diced

20g Celery, finely diced

10g Butter

100g Potatoes

500ml Fish stock

50ml Double cream

6g Fresh chives

Maldon salt and ground white pepper

Method:

1. Wash the clams well with several changes of water.
2. Place the clams into a saucepan with the fish stock and cook with a lid on the saucepan until they just begin to open. Remove from their shells and retain the stock. Strain the stock very carefully through muslin to ensure no grit is found in the stock.
3. Remove the rind of the pancetta and cut into lardons. Melt the butter and cook gently until golden brown.
4. Add the finely diced leek, onion and celery and continue to sweat with the lardons.
5. Wash, peel and cut the potatoes into 4mm dice. Add to the vegetables.
6. Add the stock and cook gently on a simmer until all vegetables are cooked – this might take approximately 20 minutes.
7. Add the clams to reheat gently and finish with the double cream. Check the consistency of the chowder and correct the seasoning. Serve with crushed water biscuits and chopped fresh chives.

Fresh North Norfolk Crab Mayonnaise on a Mandarin and Lime Jelly with Pink Grapefruit, Brown Shrimps, Dragon fruit and Tobiko

4 portions

Ingredients:

240g Freshly picked white North Norfolk crab meat

50g Brown shrimps

20 Dragon fruit cubes

20 Pink grapefruit segments

300g Mandarin purée

100g Lime juice

6g Gelatine sheets

10g Tobiko

10g Pea shoots

5g Amaranth cress, red vein sorrel, coriander, parsley cress

12 Slices Melba toast

15g Roasted nibbed almonds

10g Fresh dill

½ Juice of lemon

60g Freshly made mayonnaise

Maldon salt and ground white pepper

Method:

1. Mix the crab with the mayonnaise, almonds, lemon juice and dill and season well with salt and pepper. Place in a refrigerator to chill.

2. Warm the mandarin purée and dissolve into this 1 sheet of bloomed gelatine per 100ml of purée. Use this to flood flat service or bowl plates, and allow to set in a refrigerator. You can set herbs and or other garnish into the jelly for colour contrast.

3. Repeat the above step using the lime juice, but set into a flat tray lined with clingfilm. When set, remove from the tray and dice into very small cubes.

4. Once the jelly has set, decorate the plate with the dragon fruit, brown shrimps, pea shoots, amaranth cress, salads and lime jelly.

5. Place a 60mm ring onto the centre of the plates, place a quarter of the crab mixture into the ring; do not pack down, it should remain quite loose.

6. Remove the ring and decorate the top with brown shrimps, top with the Tobiko, arrange the Melba toast and serve.

Parsley and Garlic Risotto with Crispy Snails

2 portions

Ingredients:

Snails – 12 each (petit gris)

Kataifi pastry (enough to wrap 12 snails)

1 Egg (for egg wash)

30g Concassé tomatoes

30g Peeled broad beans (blanched)

50g King oyster mushroom (approx. 6, sliced and diced)

20g Parsley purée

15g Confit garlic purée

90g Pre-cooked white wine risotto (cooked yield)

4 Pecorino shavings

80g Butter

75ml Green herb oil

200ml Light chicken or vegetable stock

25g Grated Parmesan cheese

Maldon salt and ground white pepper

Method:

1. Season the king oyster mushrooms and brush with a little oil before grilling on a hot griddle in order to achieve a nice quadrilage finish.

2. Create an egg wash and season it well before coating each snail and wrapping carefully with the Kataifi pastry (you will want to keep some long strands aside). Set aside to chill in a refrigerator.

3. Finish the risotto by reheating it in a saucepan whilst adding the hot stock gradually to loosen the consistency. Add the confit garlic purée, sun blushed tomatoes and the sautéed, diced king oyster mushrooms. Add the parsley purée at the last minute in order to avoid discolouration.

4. Deep fry the snail parcels at the last moment in a hot fryer 190˚C.

5. At this stage you should finish the risotto with seasoning, the grated parmesan and unsalted butter.

6. Warm the broad beans and tomato concassé in a small pan.

7. Serve with the risotto on the plate and the broad beans and tomato concassé spooned over the risotto. Drizzle some herb oil around the risotto and place the snails on top (6 per portion).

Oatmeal Crusted Herring Fillets, Warm Pink Fir Apple Potato Salad, Chorizo Mayonnaise, Razor Clam Fritter

2 portions

Ingredients:

Herring fillets (pin boned) – 4 each
250g Cooked and peeled Pink Fir apple potatoes
40g Chorizo slices, small
60g Fresh mayonnaise
Razor clams – 4 each
½ Medium-sized red onion, peeled and sliced
20g Baby leaf rocket
Tomato petals from 1 plum tomato
60g Cucumber noodles
10ml White wine vinegar
5g Caster sugar
Small deep fat fryer with vegetable oil
Smoked paprika powder
100g Unsalted butter
Maldon salt and ground white pepper

For the pané:
200g Crushed oatmeal
100g Seasoned flour
4 Eggs, beaten

For the tempura batter:
100g Cornflour
150g Soft flour
10g Baking powder
Iced mineral or soda water

Method:

1. Fry the chorizo slices in a dry shallow pan. Drain off the excess oil and mix with the mayonnaise and the smoked paprika powder. Check consistency and seasoning and set aside for service.

2. Fry the red onions in the shallow pan, add the cooked, peeled and sliced potatoes. Now add the chorizo, tomato petals and the baby rocket, cook until the rocket has wilted, season well with salt and pepper. Reserve, warm until service.

3. Prepare the tempura batter by mixing all the flours together and gently adding the iced water a little at a time. Briefly stir but do not overstir the mixture.

4. Dip the razor clams immediately into the batter and deep fry in hot oil at about 180°C.

5. Pané the prepared herring fillets with the seasoned flour, beaten eggs and then the crushed oatmeal.

6. Fry the herrings in vegetable oil until golden brown on both sides, drain off the excess and add the butter. Let the butter foam and season with a little lemon juice, while basting the herring fillets with this.

7. Place the cooked herring fillets onto a clean kitchen cloth to help remove any excess fat and season the cucumber noodles with a little sugar and white wine vinegar.

8. Serve the herring fillets sitting on top of the chorizo vegetables, with the tempura razor clam on top. Roll the cucumber noodles into a ball. Dress the plate with the sauce and serve.

Chicken Pojarski with Foie Gras and Smitaine Sauce

Ingredients:

200g Minced fresh chicken leg
100ml Milk
60g Unsalted butter
50ml Double cream
50g White breadcrumbs
Grated nutmeg to taste
Maldon salt and ground white pepper

Smitaine sauce:

50g Finely chopped onion
25g Butter
80ml Dry white wine
Juice from ¼ of a lemon
150ml Sour cream
Fresh chives, chopped

Garnish:

50g Rougie foie gras
Baby spinach, washed and picked
Fresh chervil and potato press
Tomato concassé

Method:

For the pojarski:

1. Ensure that the minced chicken has been passed through the mincer twice to break the protein down.
2. Soak the breadcrumbs in the milk for a few minutes and then squeeze out any surplus milk. Add the breadcrumbs to the chicken and mix well. Season with salt, pepper and nutmeg.
3. Work in the cold double cream, a little at a time, using a spoon. Mix thoroughly and beat well.
4. Divide the mixture into equal portion sizes and mould as shown. Use some flour to help mould the shapes.

Cooking the pojarskis:

1. Heat the butter in a shallow pan and carefully place the pojarskis in hot oil to shallow fry. Fry on both sides and place into an oven until thoroughly cooked. To check, press the pojarskis gently, the juices should run clear and with no sign of blood, indicating they are cooked through.
2. Retain in a warm place for service.

To make the Smitaine sauce:

1. Place the chopped onion in a saucepan with the butter and sweat without colour. Drain off any excess fat and add the white wine. Reduce by two-thirds.
2. Add the lemon juice and then the soured cream. Continue to reduce the sauce to a coating consistency. Season well and pass through a fine sieve, add the fresh chives. Keep hot.

To cook the foie gras:

1. In a separate shallow pan quickly seal and cook the foie gras on both sides. DO NOT OVERCOOK! Season and retain for service.
2. Place the washed spinach in the same pan, season well and cook until it is wilted. Drain any excess moisture in a colander.

To serve:

1. Spoon the spinach into a stainless steel ring placed in the centre of a serving plate with the foie gras.
2. Remove the ring, position the pojarski on the spinach.
3. Spoon the Smitaine sauce around the plate.
4. Garnish with the chervil and potato press and finish with the tomato.

Guinea Fowl with Pistachio and Morel Farce, Carrot and Fois Gras Purée, Braised Potato, Buttered Spinach with Pickled Red Onions, Madeira Jus

2 portions

Ingredients:

2 Skinless and wingless guinea fowl suprêmes
50ml Vegetable oil
120g Chicken mousseline
40g Diced ham
20g Chopped and blanched pistachio nuts
20g Diced morel mushrooms
30g Finely chopped shallots
120g Peeled carrots
30g Foie Gras
Fondant potato – 2 each
1 litre Chicken stock
75ml Madeira
250g Picked baby spinach
75g Unsalted butter
Maldon salt and ground white pepper
Ground nutmeg to taste
75g Red onion, finely sliced
150ml Pickling liquid for onions (red wine vinegar, sugar, peppercorns, star anise to taste)

Method:

1. Mix the pistachio nuts, morel mushrooms and diced ham carefully with the chicken mousseline.

2. Take the guinea fowl suprêmes and butterfly cut them. Flatten with a meat bat and fill with the enriched chicken mousseline. Roll up into a log shape in clingfilm (5cm in diameter) and steam at 82˚C until each suprême is thoroughly cooked through.

3. Colour the fondant potato in some butter in a pan and top up with half the amount of the boiling chicken stock and braise in a preheated oven set at 180°C.

4. Melt the foie fras in a saucepan and retain the fat (this is to finish and enrich the carrot purée).

5. Sweat half of the chopped shallots in some vegetable oil; add the peeled and finely diced carrots. Top up with water, season and cover, cooking until the carrots are soft.

6. Drain off the water from the carrots, place into a food blender and reduce to a purée. Gradually incorporate the foie gras fat.

7. Soften the remainder of the chopped shallots in a pan with a little oil over heat without colour. Deglaze with the Madeira and reduce to a syrupy consistency. Add the remaining chicken stock and reduce this liquid until you achieve the required volume and consistency of a sauce. Pass the sauce through muslin cloth and check the seasoning before shaking a little butter into the sauce to finish it.

8. Bring the pickling liquid to the boil in a saucepan and add the sliced onions. Remove from the heat and let the onions cool down in the liquid.

9. Wilt the picked and washed spinach in a hot pan with a little butter or vegetable oil. Season with salt, pepper and nutmeg.

10. Ensure that all components are cooked and ready at the same time for the service.

11. Serve by slicing the suprême at an angle and plate this alongside the fondant potato, spinach, purée carrot, pickled red onion and the sauce.

Rump of Lamb with a Wild Mushroom Sausage and Madeira Jus

Ingredients:

4 Lamb rumps
300g Boned shoulder of lamb
50g Fresh, cleaned assorted wild mushrooms
1 Egg
100ml Double cream
50g Shallots, finely chopped
25g Fresh chopped coriander
25g Fresh chopped parsley
Sausage skins
Maldon salt and ground white wepper

Mint pesto dressing:

25g Toasted pine nuts
150ml Virgin olive oil
2 Small garlic cloves
50g Fresh spearmint
25g Fresh basil
Maldon salt to taste

Fig and onion marmalade:

125g Red onion, thinly sliced
25g Clear lavender honey
2 tbsp Red wine vinegar
3 tbsp Red wine
25g Dried figs

Madeira jus:

50g Finely chopped shallots
1 Clove garlic, finely chopped
1 Sprig thyme
¼ Bay leaf
1 tbsp Balsamic vinegar
200ml Madeira wine
400ml Strong brown lamb stock
1 tbsp Olive oil
Maldon salt and white pepper to taste

Method:

1. For the wild mushroom sausage, place the diced shoulder of lamb, chopped shallots and seasoning into a food blender. Blend together until the meat resembles a farce. Add the eggs and blend further. Slowly pour in some cream while still blending, check seasoning and consistency. Add the chopped coriander and parsley and briefly blend together.

2. Mix in the prepared, roughly chopped assorted wild mushrooms. Pipe into the soaked sausage skins to create one sausage of approximately 75-100g per portion. Leave to rest for approximately 20 minutes in the refrigerator. To cook, oil the sausage and place under a salamander, turning every few minutes until cooked through or shallow fry.

3. For the mint pesto, put the pine nuts, olive oil, garlic, basil and mint into a food processor and blend to a paste. Leave to one side and gently warm prior to service.

4. For the fig and onion marmalade, place the sliced onions, honey, vinegar and wine in a pan. Bring to the boil and gently simmer until the onions are soft. Add the chopped figs and cook very slowly to a marmalade consistency. Reserve warm for service.

5. For the Madeira jus, heat the oil in a sauteuse and add the shallots, garlic, thyme and bay leaf and cook for about 2-3 minutes, stirring frequently. Add the vinegar and continue to cook until the liquid has evaporated, then deglaze the pan with the Madeira and add the stock. Heat and simmer for 15 minutes, reducing and removing any scum that appears. Pass twice through a muslin-lined sieve and correct the seasoning and consistency.

6. Preheat an oven to 180°C. Place a black frying pan to heat on the stove and add a little oil. Season the scored rump of lamb and place into the hot fat, flat side down, to seal, turn over. Sear until golden brown on all sides. Place into the oven for approximately 10-13 minutes. (depending on the size).

7. To serve, remove the rumps of lamb from the oven. Immediately wrap in clingfilm and rest for 5 minutes. Spoon the red onion marmalade in the centre of serving plate. Remove the rumps of lamb from the clingfilm and strain any collected juices into the Madeira sauce. Carve the lamb and arrange next to the marmalade. After having grilled the sausages, cut each one in half on a slant and place on top.

Braised Neck of Mutton, Mutton Cornish Pasty and Broth, Jerusalem Artichoke Purée, Caper Braising Juices

Ingredients:

2 x Necks of mutton:

1 Neck split into 4 x 130g pieces for braising.

1 Neck split in half – 1 piece cooked in the broth and diced for the broth garnish. The other piece is used for the pasty and broth

For the braised mutton:

200g Carrots

200g Celery

200g Leek

150g Onion

50g Tomato purée

35g Flour

25ml Vegetable oil

500ml Brown mutton stock

2 Sprigs thyme

1 Bay leaf

80g Lilliput capers

Method:

For the mutton necks:

1. Bone the neck fillets, trim and cut in half (4 pieces used for braising, half a neck for the pasty, the other half for the broth).

2. Cut the vegetables into Mirepoix and reserve half for the broth. Colour the remainder with a little vegetable oil in a hot pan, roast the bones from the butchered necks and place all of these ingredients in the bottom of a heavy saucepan suitable for braising. Season the braising portions of mutton with salt and pepper, seal on all sides in a hot pan and place on top of the Mirepoix. Add a sprinkle of the flour, the tomato purée and singe in hot oven.

3. Remove from oven when a golden brown colour has been obtained and immediately deglaze the pan with 250ml brown mutton stock combining to make a thin sauce. Add the herbs and braise in oven for at least 2 hours – checking every so often and basting the sauce over the mutton.

4. When cooked, remove mutton and rest whilst retaining its temperature, strain the sauce through muslin and reduce to the required sauce consistency. Set aside to finish the caper jus for service.

For the broth:

250g Minced chicken breast

80g Pearl barley

6 Medium-sized egg whites

10g Fresh parsley, finely chopped

250ml Brown chicken stock

Method:

For the broth:

1. Add egg whites with the reserved diced Mirepoix and minced mutton and chicken, season with salt and pepper.

2. Place into a heavy bottomed pan and add 250ml brown mutton stock, 250ml brown chicken stock and pour into a large pan.

3. Tie a piece of mutton neck with string and place in the pan as this will be used for the garnish. Bring to a boiling point, stirring all the time and then leave to gently simmer for 1½ hours so that the stock can eventually clarify.

4. Meanwhile, separately cook the pearl barley in salted water, refresh under cold water and reserve to one side.

5. When the broth has clarified, ladle out the clear liquid and pass through a muslin cloth and a fine chinois. Remove the vegetables and wash under warm water and mix in with the pearl barley. Season with a little salt and pepper.

6. Prepare the final broth garnish; this is the boiled mutton neck which you have cooked in the broth, untied and sliced, plus cooked Mirepoix vegetables and cooked pearl barley. Combine this garnish with the piping hot clarified stock and add finely chopped parsley to finish the broth and place in the Marmite dishes with the lids placed on top.

For the pasty:

150g Turnips, finely diced

150g Swede, finely diced

400g Maris Piper potatoes, finely diced

50g Onion, finely sliced

250g Soft flour

75g Butter

75g Lard

50ml Double cream

3 Medium-sized egg yolks

Method:

For the Cornish pasty:

1. Finely dice the mutton neck and mince the remainder of the neck.

2. Seal off the diced mutton and add the finely diced turnip, potato, swede and finely sliced onion. Add the mince, some chopped parsley and season well with salt and pepper. Place in a refrigerator to chill.

3. Rub the sieved soft flour with the butter and lard and a pinch of salt, leave some fat pieces visible and bind with ice-cold water. Rest in a refrigerator for 15 minutes.

4. Make an egg wash for the pastry using the retained egg yolks and the double cream mixed together.

5. Roll out the pastry and cut into 4 small discs and brush some of the egg wash around the edges. Spoon the chilled pasty mixture into the centre of each disc. Fold and crimp on the top. Egg wash the whole pasty. Bake in a preheated oven at 200°C until the pasty is cooked to a golden brown colour and the inside filling is piping hot.

For the Jerusalem artichoke purée:

250g Jerusalem artichokes

100ml Double cream

1 Sprig rosemary

25g Unsalted butter

Method:

For the Jerusalem artichoke purée:

1. Wash the Jerusalem artichokes and wrap individually in foil with a small amount of salt and bake in an oven at 180°C until tender.

2, Cut in half and scoop out the insides.

3. Blend together in a Vitamix with the double cream infused with rosemary; add the unsalted butter, season and pass through a fine chinois.

For vegetable garnishes:

100g Curly kale

50ml Double cream

100g Smoked bacon

200g Baby carrots

100g Butter

5g Chopped fresh parsley

10g Caster sugar

100g Pied de Mouton mushrooms

Maldon salt and ground white pepper

Method:

For the vegetable garnishes:

1. Blanch the curly kale and refresh in iced water. Cut the smoked bacon into small dice and blanch in boiling water, also refresh and set aside. Heat a sauteuse with a small amount of oil, add the kale and bacon and finish with a little cream. Season well with salt and pepper.

2. Trim and clean the Pied de Mouton mushrooms and sauté in 50g hot butter and season, finish with chopped parsley.

3. Peel and curve the edges of the baby carrots, cook in salted and sugared water with 50g butter. When glazed toss in some chopped parsley and set aside for service.

To serve:

1. The jus is made from the cooking liquor of the braised mutton which when cooked is removed. The jus is strained, adjusted for consistency and seasoned. Add the Lilliput capers and some chopped parsley.

Braised Neck of Mutton, Mutton Cornish
Pasty and Broth, Jerusalem Artichoke
Purée, Caper Braising Juices

Pork Saltimbocca

Serves 2

Ingredients:

2 x 150g Pork escalopes
2 Slices prosciutto
4 Sage leaves
Soft flour for dusting
1 tbsp Olive oil
10g Butter
50ml Marsala wine
1 Lemon

Method:

1. Bat the pork escalopes lightly until 5mm thick.
2. Cover the pork with the slices of prosciutto. Add a leaf of sage secured with a cocktail stick.
3. Season the flour with Maldon salt and ground white pepper, and dust the pork. Shake off the excess flour.
4. Heat the oil in a shallow pan and cook escalopes for 2-3 minutes each side.
5. Set aside and keep warm in an oven. Using the same pan deglaze the cooking juices with the Marsala wine and add a good squeeze of the lemon juice.
6. Add the cold butter gently off the heat and shake in vigorously to give the sauce a good shine.
7. Serve with wilted greens and soft polenta.

Rib Eye Steak 'Vert Pre'

Ingredients:

2 x 200g Rib eye steak
1 Plum tomatoes
2 Flat mushrooms
¼ Bunch watercress
2 Egg yolks
65g Clarified butter
1 tbsp Tarragon vinegar

For the Beurre Maître d'hôtel:

¼ Bunch tarragon
1 large potato
½ tsp Peppercorns, crushed
2 tbsp Butter
2 tbsp Olive oil
Maldon salt and ground white pepper
Few drops lemon juice
100g Unsalted butter

Method:

1. To make the Beurre Maître d'hôtel for the garnish, wash, dry, and finely chop parsley. In a bowl, mix the butter, parsley and lemon juice together with a spoon until you obtain a creamy texture. Season well with salt and pepper and place on clingfilm and roll it to form a log of approximately 2cm in diameter. Store in the refrigerator or freezer until required.

2. Wash and peel the potato and cut into julienne. Wash again and dry thoroughly using a clean kitchen cloth. Deep fry at 180°C stirring gently until golden brown. Drain and season well.

3. To make the Béarnaise sauce, reduce the tarragon vinegar with 1tbsp of water and the peppercorns by half.

4. Whisk the egg yolk with the reduction liquid over a bain-marie until the ribbon stage has been obtained.

5. Slowly trickle the warm clarified butter into the egg preparation, whisking constantly until all of the butter has been incorporated and the sauce is thick and glossy. Season well with salt, pepper and a few drops of lemon juice.

6. Keep the Béarnaise sauce warm and covered until service.

7. Peel the flat mushrooms. Remove the eye from the tomato and cross the other end with a sharp knife. Cut the tomato in half and place both of these onto a lightly oiled baking sheet. Season and place softened butter onto the vegetables. Grill for 4-5 minutes. Keep warm for service.

8. Season the steak and preheat a griddle or heavy based shallow pan with the olive oil.

9. Grill or fry the rib eye steak, turning over every 30 seconds until the desired cooking point has been achieved. Rest the steak for 5-6 minutes in a warm place to relax the protein after the cooking process.

10. Chop the fresh tarragon and add to the Béarnaise sauce. Dress the plate; place the tomato half on each mushroom. Serve the Béarnaise in a small pot but also spoon a little into the centre of each grilled tomato. Garnish the steak with the straw potatoes, picked watercress and a slice of the Beurre Maître d'hôtel.

Sole Paupiette with Brown Crab and Cognac Mousse, Norfolk Asparagus, Baby Carrots, Cauliflower and Almond Purée, Glazed Jersey Pearls, Clam Beurre Blanc

Serves 2

Ingredients:

2 Lemon sole

100g Brown crab meat

5 Scallops (with skirt removed)

25ml Cognac

150ml Double cream

1 Egg white

50g Each of celery, onion, fennel, leek

1 Shallot, finely diced

6 Spears of asparagus

1 Lemon

6 Baby carrots

150g Cauliflower

5ml Almond extract

300ml Milk

50g Puff pastry

2 Cloves

1 Bay leaf

10g Dill

10g Chives

25g Tomberries

6 Clams

Red aramanth to garnish

150g Jersey pearls (depending on the season)

Maldon salt and black pepper

Method:

1. To prepare the mousseline, burn off the alcohol in the cognac by allowing it to boil and then set aside to chill. In a food processor, blitz the scallop meat, brown crab meat and egg white with a pinch of Maldon salt. Remove and place into a bowl over ice. Gradually add 100ml of double cream and finish with the zest of one lemon and finely chopped dill. Check the seasoning and place into a piping bag and the rest in the refrigerator.

2. Prepare the lemon sole by removing the gills, fins and eyes. Wash and dry the fish before cross filleting and skinning. Clean and retain the bones. In between two pieces of clingfilm bat out each fillet.

3. To make the paupiette, place the fillet presentation side down onto fresh clingfilm, season with salt and lemon juice and pipe the mousseline onto the fillet before rolling away from yourself. Wrap tightly and tie at both ends. Repeat this with all of the fillets.

4. For the fish stock, cut the celery, onion, fennel and leek into small Mirepoix and sweat in a small amount of butter. Add the clean bones and continue to sweat for 2 more minutes. Cover with water and allow to simmer for 20 minutes, skimming throughout. Pass through a chinois and muslin cloth before returning to the heat and allowing to reduce.

5. To make the cauliflower purée, cut the cauliflower into even-sized pieces. Heat a small knob of butter in a pan and sweat off. Cover with milk and add the cloves and bay leaf. When the cauliflower is tender, strain (ensuring the cloves and bay leaf are removed) and blitz in a food processor adding some of the milk until a purée consistency is achieved. Add a few drops of almond extract and season to taste. Clingfilm and set aside.

6. Cut a croute from the puff pastry and cook in between 2 trays at 180°C for 10-12 minutes, or until golden. Leave to rest on a wire rack.

7. Prepare the asparagus by removing the bottom, woody part. This can be done by bending the asparagus and allowing it to snap naturally. Turn the bottom. Blanch in boiling salted water for around 5 minutes or until 'al dente' and place into iced water. Trim the stalks and turn the baby carrots and cook in the same way as the asparagus.

8. Sweat the shallot before adding white wine and white wine vinegar and reducing. Add 200ml of the fish stock and reduce by one-third. Strain and allow simmering.

9. Remove the lemon sole from the refrigerator and poach, still wrapped in the clingfilm for 8 minutes.

10. Wash the Jersey pearls and blanch in salted boiling water for 10 minutes until tender.

11. Heat and glaze the asparagus and carrots in butter and season.

12. Glaze the potatoes in salted butter and finish with chives.

13. Remove the fish from the water and allow to rest for 2 minutes. Drain on a clean kitchen cloth before cutting the Paupiette at a diagonal angle.

14. Reheat the purée and finish the sauce by adding the clams and allowing to open, finish with cream, tomberries and adjust the seasoning if required.

Desserts

Bread and butter pudding

Ingredients:

25g Butter, plus extra for greasing

8 Thin slices white bread

50g Sultanas

2 tsp Cinnamon powder

350ml Whole milk

50ml Double cream

2 Free-range eggs

25g Granulated sugar

Nutmeg, grated, to taste

Method:

1. Grease a 1 litre pie dish with butter.

2. Cut the crusts off the white bread. Spread each slice, on 1 side, with butter and cut into triangles.

3. Arrange a layer of bread, buttered-side up, in the bottom of the dish, then add a layer of sultanas. Sprinkle with a little cinnamon, and then repeat the layers of bread and sultanas, sprinkling with a little cinnamon, until you have used up all of the bread. Finish with a layer of bread, and then set aside.

4. Gently warm the milk and cream in a saucepan over a low heat to scalding point. Don't let it boil.

5. Crack the eggs into a bowl, add three quarters of the sugar and lightly whisk until pale.

6. Add the warm milk and cream mixture and stir well, then strain the custard into a bowl.

7. Pour the custard over the prepared bread layers and sprinkle with nutmeg and the remaining sugar and leave to stand for 30 minutes.

8. Preheat the oven to 180°C.

9. Place the dish into the oven and bake for 30-40 minutes, or until the custard has set and the top is golden-brown.

10. Serve on its own or with vanilla ice cream and fresh apricot compote.

Chocolate Mousse

Makes 6-8 depending on the dish size

Ingredients:

55g Milk

70g Pasteurised egg yolks

45g Caster sugar

250g 71% Dark chocolate couverture
(Cacao Barry Fleur de Cao)

450g Whipping cream

Method:

1. Warm the milk and pour onto the egg yolks and caster sugar which have been beaten together first.

2. Return this preparation to the heat to thicken slightly, stirring with a wooden spoon all the time. Do not boil this mixture.

3. Separately melt the chocolate over a bain-marie and also aerate the whipping cream until it just holds itself in light ribbons (do not whisk too much at this point).

4. Whisk the egg yolk and milk preparation over a bowl of iced water to reduce the temperature to 30°C. Fold in the melted chocolate making sure the chocolate has not got too cold.

5. Carefully fold in the cream and pipe or spoon into the required serving dishes with the appropriate decoration.

Ginger Crème Brûlée with a Date Pudding

Ingredients for the crème brûlée:
Makes 6 individual ramekins
250ml Milk
250ml Double cream
2 Egg yolks
2 Eggs
40g Caster sugar
40ml Belvoir Ginger Cordial
1 small piece of fresh stem ginger
Stem ginger in sugar syrup

Method:
1. Preheat oven to 140°C. Finely chop 1 piece of stem ginger in sugar syrup and sprinkle a little in each of the ramekins.
2. Whisk the egg yolks, eggs and sugar together and stir in the cordial.
3. Peel the piece of fresh stem ginger, slice into large pieces and place in the pan with the milk and cream. Bring to the boil and whisk into the egg mix. Strain through a sieve into a jug.
4. Put some kitchen paper in the bottom of a roasting tray and sit the ramekins on the paper.

For a top chef's tip: place the roasting tray on the middle shelf in the oven. Slide the shelf out slightly and fill the roasting tray to within 1½cm off the top of the ramekins with hot water.

5. Pour the mix in each of the ramekins.
6. Slide the shelf carefully back into the oven and cook the crème brûlées for approximately 40 minutes.
7. The crème brûlées are cooked when they are almost set. To test, place a skewer in the middle of the crème brûlée. No liquid should run out.
8. Once cooled, scatter sugar over the top of each crème brûlée and caramelise with a blowtorch or place under a very hot grill.

For the date pudding:
Serves 12
450g Dates, pitted and diced
550ml Water
1 tsp Ground ginger
2 tsp Bicarbonate of soda
315g Self-raising flour
¼ tsp Ground cloves
¾ tsp Mixed spice
125g Unsalted butter, softened
265g Caster sugar, divided
4 Large eggs

Method:
1. Put the dates and water in a heavy based saucepan. Bring to the boil over a medium to high heat, stirring continuously with a flat-bottomed wooden spoon.
2. Remove from the heat and add ginger and bicarbonate of soda. Stir until well combined. Let the mixture cool to room temperature.
3. Preheat oven to 180°C.
4. Sieve together the self-raising flour, ground cloves and mixed spice.
5. In a separate bowl, cream the butter for 1-2 minutes. Add half the caster sugar and beat for 2 minutes. Add the remaining caster sugar and beat for 2 minutes or until light and fluffy.
6. Add the eggs, one at a time, beating for 1 minute after each addition or until the mixture is light and fluffy. Use a rubber spatula to fold in the flour mixture until well combined.
7. Fold in the cool date mixture until thoroughly combined.
8. Spoon the mixture into moulds or greased tins, filling each a little more than three-quarters full.
9. Bake in the oven for about 35-40 minutes, or until they spring back when touched lightly in the middle.

For the Butterscotch Sauce:
165g Dark brown soft sugar
125g Unsalted butter, cubed
300ml Extra-thick double cream

To serve:
1. For the small toffee apple, drain and dry cherry apples, then dip in hot caramel and leave to set on a cold and oiled marble slab.
2. Serve the crème brûlée in the centre of a plate with a piece of the date pudding next to it with the butterscotch sauce poured over it.

Lemon Tart with Autumn Berry Compote

Ingredients:

For the Sweet Paste:

510g Soft flour

340g Butter diced

170g Caster sugar infused with vanilla

1 Egg

100ml Double cream

Method:

1. Rub together the chilled butter and flour to a crumb texture.
2. Add caster sugar.
3. Combine the egg and cream and add to the mix.
4. Carefully create a smooth paste. Cover and leave in the refrigerator to rest for 30 minutes.
5. Roll out and line a suitable flan ring and bake blind in a preheated oven set at 180°C.

For the Lemon Tart filling:

4 Lemons juice and finely grated zest

6 Whole eggs

150g Caster Sugar

375g Double cream

Method:

1. Whisk together the eggs and caster sugar, add the juice and zest, but try not to aerate the mixture.
2. Add the double cream and mix well.
3. Fill the pre-baked flan case to just under the rim and bake at 160°C until just set.
4. Cool to room temperature.

For the fruit compote:

700g Mixed summer berries, e.g. blackcurrants, raspberries, red currants, white currants, blueberries, blackberries

250g Caster sugar

125ml Red wine

1 Sprig rosemary

1 Vanilla pod, split open

Method:

1. Place the fruit in a saucepan and add the sugar, wine, rosemary and split vanilla pod. Use a saucepan made of a metal that does not react to high acidic fruits (such as aluminium).
2. Bring to the boil and stir until the sugar has dissolved. Turn down the heat and simmer for 1 minute. Remove from the heat.
3. When the compote has cooled, remove the vanilla pod and rosemary and serve.

Sticky Toffee Pudding with Clotted Cream Ice Cream

Serves 6-8

Ingredients:

175g Chopped dates
300ml Water
1 tsp Bicarbonate of soda
50g Unsalted butter
175g Soft dark brown sugar
2 Eggs
175g Self raising flour
1 tsp Natural vanilla flavour

Method:

1. Grease well the dariole moulds or a large dish with soft butter.
2. Cover the chopped dates with water and cook until soft.
3. Cream together the butter and sugar until soft. Gradually add the eggs and beat well.
4. Add the sieved bicarbonate of soda to the dates. They will turn slightly frothy but gradually add to the base preparation.
5. Add the flour and vanilla.
6. Use the mix as required. Either individually pipe into moulds or spoon into a dish. Do not over fill containers because the mix will rise quite a lot.
7. Bake for approximately 25 minutes in a preheated oven set 180°C until firm to the touch.

For the toffee sauce:

50g Butter
150g Soft brown sugar (use light or dark depending on end colour required)
50g Caster sugar
150ml Golden syrup
150ml Double cream

Method:

1. Put all of the ingredients onto a low heat, in a saucepan, and bring to the boil ensuring that the sugar is dissolved. Remove from heat.
2. Add the double cream and a few drops of vanilla flavour.
3. This sauce is now ready to use, and will also keep for quite a while in the refrigerator.

For the clotted cream ice cream:

300ml Clotted cream
150ml Milk
5 Free-range egg yolks
115g Caster sugar

Method:

1. Place the cream and milk in a saucepan and heat gently until on the verge of boiling.
2. Meanwhile, whisk the egg yolks with the sugar in a large bowl until well combined.
3. Slowly add the hot cream mixture, continuing to whisk as you do so.
4. Pour the mixture back into the saucepan and cook over a low heat, stirring constantly, until thick enough to coat the back of a wooden spoon. Be careful not to let the mixture get too hot or it might split.
5. Pass through a fine sieve and allow to cool completely.
6. Churn in an ice-cream machine to a soft consistency.
7. Transfer to an airtight container and put into the freezer for at least 2 hours.
8. Take out of the freezer 15 minutes before serving.

The Baroness Burdett-Coutts Cocktail

The Escoffier

Cocktails

The Peach Melba Cocktail

The Peach Melba is a classic dessert, invented in the early 1890s by the French chef and co-founder of Westminster, Auguste Escoffier at the Savoy Hotel, London. Escoffier designed it to honour the Australian soprano, Nellie Melba. It combines two popular summer fruits: peaches and raspberries with an accompanying vanilla ice cream.

Ingredients:

2 parts Bols peach liqueur
1 part Peach purée
1 part Double cream
Raspberry caviar pearls

Method:

1. To make the raspberry caviar pearls, purée fresh raspberries in a Vitamix and strain through muslin cloth to obtain a pure raspberry juice. Add 2g agar to 100ml of the juice and heat up to 80°C stirring constantly.
2. Remove from the heat, fill a pipette with the raspberry liquid and drop beads into very cold vegetable oil. Sieve oil to retrieve the beads, rinse out the oil with water in a sieve.

Science tip: When making gelled beads with acidic ingredients, use agar instead of alginate. When making solutions with acidic ingredients such as raspberry, the sodium alginate will start to gel prematurely.

3. Add to the base of the drink.
4. Shake the peach liqueur, peach purée and double cream over ice and strain into a chilled Martini glass with the raspberry caviar pearls at the bottom.

White Lady (The Baroness Burdett-Coutts Cocktail)

This is a simple but lovely classic drink with a sour finish, originally created in 1919 by Harry MacElhone, when he was working at Ciro's Club, London, England. Nowadays the White Lady is considered the archetypal cocktail associated with the Savoy Hotel. However, we have worked on an adaption of this as a dedication to Westminster Kingsway College's very own 'white lady' – our benefactor Baroness Burdett-Coutts.

Ingredients:

1¾ shots Bombay London dry gin
1 shot Cointreau triple sec
1 shot Freshly squeezed lemon juice
1 Pasteurised egg white

Method:

1. Shake all the ingredients with ice and fine strain into a chilled Martini glass.
2. Garnish with a lemon zest twist and serve.

See picture on page 116.

The Peach Melba Cocktail

Canapés & Savouries

Blood Orange and Foie Gras Macaroons

Ingredients:

For the Foie Gras:
300g Trimmed and deveined foie gras

20ml Sherry

1 Pinch ground cloves

1 Shallot, finely chopped

5 Juniper berries

½ tsp Maldon sea salt

Ground white pepper

Method:
1. Place all of the ingredients except the shallots and salt into a vacuum bag and seal to leave overnight in a refrigerator.
2. Drain off the liquid content from the sealed bag and remove the juniper berries.
3. Pan-fry in a hot pan, add the shallots, season and then rest for 5 minutes.
4. Place into a high speed blender, slowly adding the cream to create a smooth piping consistency.

For the blood orange jelly:
250ml Blood orange juice

2 Gelatine leaves

Juice of ½ lemon

25ml Mineral water

15g Caster sugar

Method:
1. Bloom the gelatine in cold water.
2. Mix the orange and lemon juices together with the mineral water and caster sugar in a pan.
3. Bring to the boil then remove from the heat. Remove any excess impurities from the surface of the liquid.
4. Squeeze the excess water from the gelatine and whisk into the juice.
5. Pass the liquid through a fine sieve and pour into a tray to chill and set in a refrigerator.
6. Once it has completely set into a jelly, cut into small squares or small discs and reserve to one side.

For the macaroons:
Stage 1

130g Ground almonds

130g Icing sugar

50g Egg white

Powdered orange colour

Stage 2

200g Granulated sugar

65g Water

55g Caster sugar

90g Egg whites

1g Albumen powder

Method:
1. Preheat oven to 160°C.
2. Prepare the baking trays for piping.
3. Sieve the almonds and icing sugar from 'stage 1' and add the egg white and colour to form a stiff paste.
4. Whisk the whites from 'stage 2' and gradually add the caster sugar and albumen powder to form soft peaks that just hold together.
5. Mix the water and granulated sugar and boil to 120°C.
6. Pour in the sugar syrup to the aerated egg whites to create an Italian meringue.
7. Carefully fold a third of the meringue into the paste from 'stage 1' and repeat twice more until the meringue has been successfully folded into the mixture.
8. Using a plain tube, pipe onto prepared trays.
9. Bang or knock the baking tray a couple of times, and set aside in a cool place to let the macaroons skin over. This will take approximately 40 minutes.
10. Place in the preheated oven to bake for 10 minutes, then open the oven door and bake for a further 15–20 minutes until the macaroons have dried out.

To Assemble:
1. Select pairs of macaroons the same sizes as each other.
2. Pipe the foie gras onto 1 macaroon, and press a square or disc of jelly on top and place the other macaroon shell on top.
3. Finish if desired with a little gold leaf or a little dusting of food grade colouring.

Deconstructed Welsh Rarebit
4-6 portions

Ingredients:

4 White bread

100g Clarified butter

250ml Béchamel sauce

150g Gloucestershire cheese

For the Worcestershire jelly:

500ml Beef stock

1 Shallot, finely chopped

50ml Port

4 Black peppercorns

1 Sprig thyme

100ml Ale, such as Fuller's London Porter

1 tsp English mustard

1 pinch Cayenne pepper

1 tsp Redcurrant jelly

6g Agar

Worcestershire sauce

Method:

1. Cut the crusts off of the bread and roll thinly but carefully so as not to break the bread. Trim the sides and cut each piece into 4 squares.

2. Brush with clarified butter. Roll around a metal rod and press the sides together to form a cylinder.

3. Bake in a preheated oven until crisp, then set aside and lightly dust with Cayenne pepper.

For the jelly:

1. Sweat off the shallots with the thyme and peppercorns.

2. Add the Port and ale and then reduce to small amount.

3. Hydrate the agar in cold water until soft then drain off the excess water.

4. Add the redcurrant jelly, mustard and a good dash of Worcestershire sauce. Add the agar and simmer for 2 minutes.

5. Pass through a fine sieve, pour onto a tray and set in a refrigerator.

Finish and presentation:

1. Add the cheese to the hot béchamel. The sauce should be of a double cream consistency.

2. Place the mixture into an ISI Thermo-Whip and charge with 3 gas cartridges.

3. Cut the jelly into small cubes.

4. Squirt cheese mousse/foam into a bowl. Fold in jelly and then pipe mix into toasted bread cylinders.

5. Serve warm.

Tomato and Garlic Caviar Spheres

Ingredients:

250g Tomato juice

5g Garlic paste

5g Agar

200ml Very cold vegetable oil

Method:

1. Heat the tomato juice, garlic paste and agar until the mixture is boiling.
2. Fill a pipette with the hot liquid, and drop beads into the cold oil.
3. The beads should solidify as they fall to the bottom of the oil.
4. Rinse the beads with water before serving.

Deep Fried Pork Belly Rillette with a Piccalilli Foam, Apple Caviar Salad

4 portions

Ingredients:

1kg Boneless pork belly, cut into squares
60ml Apple brandy
1 tbsp Maldon sea salt
3 Sprigs of thyme
2 Bay leaves
2 Juniper berries
8 Black peppercorns
250ml Duck fat
500ml Pork, chicken or veal stock
2 tbsp Flat parsley
150g Chopped cornichons
150g Chopped washed capers
Pané – plain seasoned flour, egg wash, airbag pork, Panko breadcrumbs

Method:

1. Preheat oven to 150°C. Cut the meat in to small pieces.
2. In a mortar and pestle; grind up the bay, thyme, salt, peppercorns and juniper berries.
3. Put the meat in a large bowl and pour over the brandy. Add the spices and toss really well to combine. Cover the bowl, and place it in a refrigerator overnight.
In a heavy large pan, heat up a couple of tablespoons of the fat. Toss in the meat and brown lightly. Add the rest of the fat, and let it melt.
4. Pour in enough stock to almost cover the meat. Cover with tin foil and place in the oven for about 3 hours.
5. Stir throughout the cooking process. If the liquid level looks to be too low, add a little more to keep the level topped up.
6. After 3 hours remove the meat from the cooking liquid. Let the meat cool just enough to handle. Pull the meat apart with your fingers. Bind with some of the cooking liquid, 1 tablespoon at a time to the meat. You want the meat to be moist and tacky.
7. Add the chopped parsley, capers and cornichons to the meat, and mix.
8. Mould the rillette into equal size balls, 1 per portion and then chill to firm the meat up.
9. Meanwhile make the pané mix and coat the chilled rillettes, leave at room temperature for at least half an hour before frying.

For the piccalilli foam:

1 Small cauliflower
1 Red pepper
1 Cucumber
500g Silverskin onions
200g Sugar
250g White wine vinegar
250g Water
2 tbsp Maldon salt
1 tbsp English mustard
1 tsp Turmeric
½ tsp Ground ginger
2 tsp Brown mustard seeds
80g Cornflour

Method:

1. Cut the vegetables into small equal sized pieces and place into the water, then add the salt and leave overnight.
2. Wash off and drain
3. Boil the vinegar, sugar and mustard seeds together and cook the drained vegetables. Reserve the water and save some of the vegetables for garnishing the finished dish.
4. Mix the ginger, English mustard, turmeric and cornflour together with a little cold water to form a paste then gradually add the hot cooking water. Place it back onto the stove to thicken stirring continuously.
5. Place the vegetables into a high speed blender and gradually add the thickened liquid until smooth add a little stock or water to loosen if needed. Pour the mixture into an ISI Thermo-Whip and charge with 3 gas cartridges.

For the apple caviar salad:
1 Punnet baby watercress
Thin slices of radish
25ml Apple cider vinegar
75ml English rapeseed oil
4 Crushed white peppercorns
1 Brunoise of a green apple
225g Apple juice
1.8g Sodium alginate
½ tsp Cinnamon
500g Water
2.5g Calcium chloride

Method:
1. Mix the sodium alginate with the apple juice using an immersion blender until the sodium alginate is completely dissolved. Then immediately heat the mixture to 96°C before quickly chilling rapidly and cover.
2. Prepare the calcium bath in a bowl by dissolving the calcium chloride in the water.
3. Add the apple-alginate mixture to a caviar-maker tray and follow the manufacturer's instructions. Alternately you can use a syringe and directly syringe droplets into the calcium bath.
4. After a minute, remove the apple caviar from the calcium bath, rinse in clean water.
5. Mix the salad ingredients together and dress with apple cider vinegar and English rapeseed oil, add the caviar and season with white peppercorns and sea salt.

To Serve:
1. Deep fry the rillette balls until hot and golden in colour.
2. Squirt the piccalilli onto the plate, top with the rillette ball.
3. Arrange the salad and remaining reserved piccalilli vegetables.

Terrine of Foie Gras and Artichokes

Makes one terrine

First Stage Ingredients:

775g Foie gras escalopes

200g Curing salt

200g Caster sugar

50g Crushed black pepper, roasted and cooled

Method:

1. Mix the curing salt, sugar and pepper together.
2. Sprinkle a layer on the bottom of a clean tray.
3. Place on the frozen foie gras escalopes and cover with the remaining salt/sugar/pepper mix.
4. Cover and allow to defrost completely, or for 4 hours, this will cure the foie gras to the correct degree. Place in a refrigerator.
5. Wash off the cure with cold running water, and using fish tweezers, remove any veins by grasping around the exposed vein and carefully pulling until the vein comes out. Repeat this process with all the escalopes, and then chill in a refrigerator until they have firmed.

Second Stage Ingredients:

Prepared foie gras from the first stage

100ml Sauternes

Vacuum bags

250g Jerusalem artichokes, peeled, shaped into cylinders, and roasted

4 Artichokes, peeled turned, cooked in a blanc, quartered and roasted

200ml Chicken glace stock

Maldon salt and ground white pepper

1 x 1kg terrine mould, oiled and lined with clingfilm

Method:

1. Place the foie gras escalopes (grouped in 6 per bag) into vacuum bags with some sauternes and seal on the highest setting (normally 1) on the vacuum machine and place back into the refrigerator until ready to cook Sous Vide.
2. Set a sous vide machine to 55°C, carefully place the foie gras to cook for 30 minutes.
3. Cut the bags and tip out onto a tray. Trim the foie gras neatly to form rectangular slabs. Save the trim to use as filler for any gaps. Layer the foie gras with the artichokes in the terrine moulds, ensuring that the chicken glace is used as binding between the layers to hold everything together. Season well between each layer.
4. The final layer should be of foie gras. Press firmly down to expel any air pockets.
5. Make a cartouche of cardboard wrapped in foil and then clingfilm, ensuring that this fits the top of the terrine precisely.
6. Use a second terrine mould or weights to weigh down the terrine and place in the refrigerator for 12 hours minimum.
7. Once set, pull the terrine from its mould using the clingfilm you lined it with, re-wrap with at least 3 layers of clingfilm and place back into the refrigerator for service.

For service (4 portions):

4 Slices terrine (approximately 60g per portion)

150g Braised lentils

30g Baby amaranth cress

50g Chopped parsley

For the sherry vinaigrette:

25ml Reduced sherry vinegar (from 100ml)

25ml Chicken glace stock

50ml Olive oil

Maldon salt and ground white pepper

Method:

1. Slice the terrine and press some of the chopped parsley around the edges.
2. Place a slice of terrine in the middle of a service plate.
3. Combine all the ingredients for the sherry vinaigrette – this is a split dressing. Taste and correct seasoning.
4. Add half of the vinaigrette to the lentils to moisten and place a cordon of lentils around the terrine.
5. Dress the baby amaranth cress with a touch of the vinaigrette, and place on and around the lentils and terrine. Drizzle around the remaining vinaigrette and serve.

Jellied French Onion Soup Consommé, Truffled Quail Eggs, Parmesan and Brioche Crumb, Chive Flowers, Baby Onion Petals

Ingredients:

3 litres Cold beef stock

1 Bottle red wine

300g Shin of beef, minced or finely chopped

5 Small onions, peeled and cut in half

20ml Olive oil

1 Stick of celery, roughly chopped

½ Medium leek, roughly chopped

3 Sprigs of thyme

1 tsp Tomato purée

10 Leaves gelatine

Maldon salt and ground white pepper

2 Egg whites

Method:

1. Finely chop the vegetables except for the half onions in a food processor with the thyme and tomato purée.

2. Add the beef and egg white and whisk well with the cold stock in a saucepan. Slowly caramelise the half onions in a little olive oil until quite dark and add these to the stock.

3. Bring to a simmer, stirring continuously until it reaches simmering point.

4. As it comes up to a simmer, the egg white and meat mixture will form a solid crust at the top of the pot. At this stage scoop a small breathing hole out and do not be tempted to stir it, leave it to simmer very gently for an hour.

5. Carefully strain the consommé through a strainer lined with muslin.

6. Place the gelatine into cold water until it is soft then add to the hot consommé.

7. Stir until dissolved then pour onto a tray and refrigerate.

For the Gruyere emulsion:

250g Gruyere cheese

4 Free-range egg yolks

2 tsp Ready-prepared English mustard

1 tbsp White wine vinegar

570ml Grapeseed oil

Maldon salt and ground white pepper

Pinch of cayenne pepper

To make the emulsion:

1. Chop the Gruyere cheese into small pieces and place into a Pacojet container. Freeze overnight and then blend in the Pacojet to form a powder.

2. Using a food processor, place the egg yolks into the bowl. Add the vinegar, salt and pepper and the mustard. Blend by 'pulsing' the food blender to commence with.

3. Maintaining the food processor on and, with the motor running, add the oil in a thin, steady stream through the top of the lid. After a minute or two, the mixture will change to a thick mayonnaise consistency.

4. Add the Gruyere powder until a good cheese flavour forms in the sauce, add a pinch of cayenne pepper and place into a plastic squeeze bottle.

For the garnish:

3 Quails eggs per portion

1 Baby onion or small shallot per person

Truffle shavings

Truffle oil

Toasted brioche crumb

To serve:

1. Blanch the baby onions and strip off each layer and char grill the 'petals'.

2. Poach the quail eggs so that they can be served warm and then drizzle over with a little truffle oil.

3. Arrange the different components on the plate and serve.

Scallops with Pea Panna Cotta and Parmigiano Reggiano Purée

Ingredients:

For the pea panna cotta:

40g shallots, chopped

Olive oil

40g butter

200g frozen peas

1 bunch of mint

40g Grated Parmigiano Reggiano,

40g Shallots, chopped

300ml Vegetable stock

1% dosage Iota Carrageenan

For the Parmigiano Reggiano purée:

300ml Milk

Parmigiano Reggiano rind

20g Butter

20g Soft flour

200g Grated Parmigiano Reggiano,

1tsp English mustard

Maldon salt and ground white pepper

For the scallops:

6 large scallops cut in half

40g Butter

To serve:

200g Finely grated Parmigiano Reggiano, grated

12 Smoked pancetta slices

Pea shoots, to garnish:

Mixed fresh herbs

Vegetable oil, for frying

Maldon salt and ground white pepper

Method:

For the panna cotta:

1. Sweat the shallots in the oil and butter. Add the peas, mint and stock, and cook for 2 minutes. Add the Parmigiano Reggiano and mix. Cool down for a few minutes and blend in a food blender. Pass through a fine sieve.

2. Add 1% of Iota Carrageenan to the liquid and slowly bring to the boil whisking continuously. Pour into oiled moulds and leave to set in a refrigerator.

For the purée:

1. Infuse the boiling milk with the Parmigiano Reggiano rind. Melt the butter and carefully stir in the soft flour. Cook for 2 minutes to bind the ingredients together and slowly add the milk, stirring all the time. Add the Parmigiano Reggiano, English mustard and check the seasoning.

For the scallops:

1. Season the scallops. Heat a shallow pan and add a little oil. Cook each side of the scallops for 2 minutes. Finish with butter, basting the scallops continuously and then drain.

To serve:

1. Place a chef's ring onto a tray with a silicone mat. Grate a little Parmigiano Reggiano into each ring and bake until golden. Remove from the oven and curl over a rolling pin. Cook the pancetta until crispy, remove from the oven and cool quickly before crushing into small pieces.

2. Season and dress the pea shoots in oil. Drag the purée along the plate and top with the de-moulded panna cotta. Place the scallops alongside the panna cotta.

3. Dress the plate with herb oil and pea shoots. Sprinkle over Parmigiano Reggiano, add the crisp and pancetta crumbs.

Butter Poached Lobster, Mango Emulsion and Coconut Bisque Foam

Serves 4

Ingredients:

2 Native lobsters

*For the lemon vinaigrette
(whisk the following ingredients
together to dress lobster):*

10g Lemon juice

10g Water

50g Rapeseed oil

15g Caster sugar

4g Maldon salt

Method:

1. Steep the lobsters by placing each one into a tight fitting heat-proof container and cover with cold water. Drain off the water, measure it and place in a large pan to boil adding 125ml of vinegar for every litre of water. Pour the water over the lobster and cover for 2-3 minutes.
2. Remove the lobsters but do not discard the water.
3. Remove the tails by twisting and pulling off. Use the same method to remove each claw and return to the water for another 5 minutes.
4. Keep the lobster carcass for the foam recipe.
5. Cut the lobsters to the size required and gently poach in clarified butter for 4 minutes when ready for service.

Coconut bisque foam:

Lobster shells from the 2 native lobsters

1 tbsp Olive oil

1 Carrot

1 Shallot

1 Clove garlic

1 Stick celery

1 Stick lemon grass finely chopped

1 Knob ginger chopped finely

1 Small red chilli

100g Leek

1 x 250g tin Unsweetened coconut cream

1 tsp Tomato purée

25ml Brandy

25ml White wine

½ tsp Powder lecithin

Lime juice to taste

Method:

1. Fry the lobster shells with a little olive oil in a hot pan until they have a good colour.
2. Roughly chop the carrot, shallot, celery and leek. Add this to the lobster shells and continue cooking until a good colour forms with the vegetables.
3. Add the brandy and flambé then add the wine and reduce by half.
4. Stir in the tomato purée and then the coconut cream with the crushed garlic, ginger, chilli and lemon grass.
5. Simmer gently until reduced to the correct sauce consistency. Finish with a little lime juice and season.
6. Pass through a fine chinois and then add ½ tsp powdered lecithin. Using a hand blender, blend the sauce to produce a stable foam.

For the passion fruit purée sheet:

500g Passion fruit purée

50g Water

100g Caster sugar

3 Gelatine leaves

Method:

1. Gently heat the purée, water and sugar until the sugar dissolves completely. Stir from time to time.
2. Hydrate the gelatine in cold water and then squeeze out the excess water. Melt into the hot purée mix and strain through a fine chinois.
3. Spread onto acetate and chill in a refrigerator. Cut as required for the dish.

For the mango emulsion:

1 Mango, skinned and stone removed

5g Maldon salt

8g Agar

Method:

1. Blend the mango in the Thermomix.

2. In a saucepan bring 500g of the mango purée, salt and agar to the boil and whisk continuously for 1½ minutes.

3. Pass through chinois and set in blast-chiller.

4. When set, blend on high speed until smooth. Strain through a fine chinois and transfer to a plastic squeeze bottle and reserve for service.

Garnish and presentation:

Kiwi

Toasted coconut strips

Lemon cress

Basil cress

Coriander cress

To serve:

1. Arrange all the prepared components on a suitable plate. The lobster can be served hot or cold.

Cured and Butter Poached Sea Bass and Frozen Saint Germain Royale

Ingredients:

For the Royale:

300g Peas

25g Chervil

25g Mint

100g Double cream

Method:

1. Blanch the peas, chervil and mint and drain.
2. Blend in a Vitamix to a purée.
3. Boil the cream and add gradually to the pea purée and continue to blend to a mousse consistency.
4. Place into a piping bag and pipe long strips onto a pre-chilled tray lined with a siliconee mat and freeze for 40 minutes.

For the Sea Bass:

2 Sea bass

1 Lemon, juice and zest

Maldon salt and black pepper

20g Olive oil

350g Melted clarified butter

For the garnish:

Dressed leaves of pea shoots and fennel

Method:

1. Scale, clean and fillet the sea bass and remove the skin off each of the fillets, season with salt and leave in a refrigerator for 20 minutes. Retain the skin from the fish.
2. Portion the remaining fillets into 4 and score the skin with a sharp knife.
3. Wash the salted fillets and skin and pat dry.
4. Lightly oil the skin and place between 2 baking sheets lined with siliconee paper. Place into a preheated oven at 180°C for approximately 8 minutes until the skin is crisp and set aside.
5. Using the salted fillets, cut into a small dice, press, season with lemon juice and zest and place into small rings and chill in refrigerator.
6. Poach the portioned fillets in the hot clarified butter for 6 minutes. Be careful to not let the butter get too hot.

To serve:

1. Place the moulded lemon-cured fish on a service plate and top with the frozen royale sticks.
2. Add the dressed leaves and crispy skin and finally the poached sea bass.

Fillets of Dover Sole 'Dugleré'

4 Portions

Ingredients:

2 Soles, skinned and filleted. Bones reserved for the sauce

1 litre Fish stock

100ml White wine

200ml Double cream

1 Clove garlic finely chopped

40g Shallots, finely chopped. Reserve the trimmings for the sauce

50g Butter

150g Puff pastry

100g Parsley, picked and washed

50g Spinach, picked and washed

50ml Tomato juice

Tomato and garlic caviar spheres

Maldon salt and ground white pepper

Method:

1. Remove the gills and eyes from the sole and discard. Remove the bones. Wash and chop into a usable size. Sweat off the reserved shallot trimmings until soft, add the bones and allow to sweat in a covered pan for a few moments, cover with the fish stock and bring to a gentle simmer skimming as required. Allow to cook and infuse for 20 minutes.

2. Using the puff pastry, cut fish shape fleurons, egg wash and bake in a preheated oven and reserve to one side for service.

3. Blanch and refresh the parsley and spinach, place into a Thermomix and blend to a fine purée. Season and pass through a fine chinois. Reserve warm.

4. Butter a pan and sprinkle with 10g of the chopped shallots and half of the chopped garlic, place the seasoned sole fillets on top and cover with 50ml white wine and some of the fish stock. Cover with a buttered paper and poach in the oven until just under cooked.

5. In a pan sweat off the remaining shallots and garlic in butter until soft. Add the white wine and reduce to half, add the fish stock, tomato juice and the cooking liquor from the fillets and reduce to a glaze consistency. Add the cream, reduce to the correct consistency, season, pass through a chinois and reserve hot. When required, whisk with a hand blender to create a foamy sauce.

6. To plate the dish, dress the plates with a brush of parsley, arrange the fillets neatly on top of the spinach, sauce over with the foam and garnish with the tomato spheres around. Finish with a fleuron and serve.

Roast Fillet of John Dory Nettle Gnocchi and New Season Peas, Marjoram Oil

Serves 4

Ingredients:

2 John Dory (400g-500g, filleted and skinned)

For the sauce:

100g White Mirepoix
20ml Noilly Pratt
Double cream
30g Butter
Maldon salt and ground white pepper

For the marjoram oil:

1 Bunch of marjoram
100ml Vegetable oil

For the gnocchi:

125g Red skin potatoes (baked)
40g "00" flour
5g Grated Parmesan cheese
100g Nettles blanched (no stalks)
30g Crushed wild garlic (or 20g garlic clove)
1 Egg yolk
Maldon salt and ground white pepper

For the garnish:

150g Shelled and cooked peas
4 Fried nettle leaves
20g Butter
Maldon salt and ground white pepper

Method:

1. Prepare the sauce by softening the Mirepoix in butter and adding the Noilly Pratt and the bones from the filleted fish.

2. Add 1 litre of water, season and simmer for 20 minutes carefully reducing by half. Add the cream and again reduce until the correct consistency is achieved

3. Prepare the gnocchi by scooping the flesh out of the freshly baked potato and adding the rest of the ingredients carefully forming a soft and warm dough.

4. Roll into a sausage shape and cut into small pieces and roll and form on the back of a fork. Blanch in salted simmering water.

5. Blend the marjoram with the vegetable oil and hang in muslin over a clean bowl to catch the oil.

6. Deep fry the nettle leaves until they are crisp and re-heat the peas in the butter and season, keep warm.

To serve:

1. Season the John Dory fillets, add butter into a non-stick frying pan and sear on both sides until a light golden brown colour is formed and the fish is cooked. Keep warm.

2. Divide and place the gnocchi and peas into 4 warm bowls, place the John Dory fillets on top, foam the warm fish cream sauce with a hand blender and pour around.

3. Garnish with the fried nettles and marjoram oil.

Monkfish and Red Mullet Bourride

Ingredients:

60g Pieces monkfish tail

60g Red mullet fillets, each

500g Lobster shells, chopped into small pieces

50g Unsalted butter

20ml Vegetable oil

20ml Cognac

50ml White wine

50ml Noilly Pratt

5g Fennel seeds

1 Bay leaf

1 Star anise

1 Sprig of thyme

5g Tomato purée

1 Crushed clove of garlic

50g Shallots, sliced

1 tbsp Chopped parsley and chervil

500ml Fish stock

1 Egg yolk

80ml Olive oil

1 Pinch saffron

4 Baby carrots

4 Baby leeks

40g Broad beans, double shelled

Method:

1. Sweat the lobster shells in butter and oil until lightly coloured, add the chopped shallots and garlic.

2. Add the tomato purée and cook for a further 5 minutes.

3. Pour in the Cognac and flame to burn off the alcohol. Add the wine and Noilly Pratt and cook out for another 2 minutes.

4. Add the fish stock, fennel seeds and saffron and simmer for 20 minutes.

5. Pass through a fine chinois and the press the shells.

6. Pour into a clean pan and keep warm.

7. Place an egg yolk into a glass bowl and whisk with 5ml warm water. Emulsify by gradually adding the olive oil in a similar process as making fresh mayonnaise.

8. Gently heat the liquid and whisk in the egg and oil mix until it has thickened. At this point it is essential to not boil this preparation.

9. Finish by adding the chopped fresh herbs.

10. Grill the mullet and pan fry the monkfish. Rest the fish for a few seconds and arrange into bowl plates. Pour the bourride over.

11. Garnish with glazed baby leeks, carrots and broad beans.

Canard à la Presse

Serves 4

Ingredients:

2 Large ducks (1.6kg each)

1 Measure of PX Sherry

1 Small glass of Cognac

1 Glass of well seasoned duck
consommé or veal stock

50g Foie gras

Juice of ½ lemon

50g Clarified butter

Maldon salt and ground white pepper

Method:

1. Roast both ducks in a hot oven for 20-30 minutes. The kitchen team must prepare the ducks by removing the breasts from each duck and presenting them for the restaurant team to finish.

2. Also remove the duck legs and gently grill them in the kitchen, whilst the restaurant team are preparing the duck fillets à la Guéridon. Timing between the kitchen and restaurant teams is essential.

3. In the restaurant, in front of the guests; remove the skin off the duck fillets and slice them thinly, but as wide as possible.

4. Begin to cook the fillets of the duck breast in the clarified butter and then flambé with the Cognac.

5. Cut the remaining duck carcass with large scissors and place in the Duck Presse in order to crush and remove as much blood and juices from the duck as possible.

6. Add the duck consommé or veal stock to the duck fillets as well as the sherry, lemon, blood juices from the carcass, seasoned with salt and pepper and let the sauce reduce for 10-15 minutes (keep mixing at all times)

7. Add the foie gras to *monter* the sauce, to give it a shine and a rich, smooth finish. Plate the duck fillets onto hot plates and napper with a generous amount of the sauce.

8. Serve traditionally with Pommes Soufflées, or in this case, with Pommes Château.

9. Bring in a second service, the grilled duck legs served with a simple, dressed green salad.

Duck à L'Orange, Duck Skin 'Crumb', Orange 'Spheres' and an Orange and Grand Marnier Jus

Ingredients:

2 Gressingham ducks, legs and breasts with skin removed

1 Bay leaf

4 Black peppercorns

50g Shallots, finely chopped

1 Clove garlic

1 Stick celery, finely diced

1 Carrot, finely diced

3 Oranges

5 Sprigs thyme

300ml Orange juice made up with juice from the oranges plus extra if needed

50ml Grand Marnier

200ml Veal jus

200ml Duck stock

100g Butter

15ml Oil

25g Sugar

Maldon salt and ground white pepper

For the orange spheres:

200ml Freshly squeezed orange juice

150ml Duck stock

1.2g Sodium alginate

1g Calcium chloride

Method:

1. The day before needed, season the legs with salt and pepper and place in a vacuum bag with a sprig of thyme. Cook for 12 hours at 70°C, chill, flake and reserve until required.

2. Chop the carcasses and brown in a hot oven. Remove excess fat and place into a clean pan. Cover with the stock and jus and bring to a simmer. Cook for 30 minutes, skimming as required. Pass through a muslin cloth and reserve.

3. Zest the oranges, save a piece for the duck breasts and cut the remainder into a fine julienne, blanch and refresh twice, put into a clean pan, add the sugar and enough water to cover and allow to cook to a light syrup, reserve. Juice the oranges for the sauce.

4. Freeze the duck skins in liquid nitrogen*, and then blend to a fine crumb using a food blender. Place 5ml oil in a non-stick frying pan and cook until crisp and golden in colour, season and reserve in an air tight container.

5. Place duck breasts in a vacuum bag with salt, pepper, a sprig of thyme and reserved piece of orange zest, cook for 25 minutes at 60°C.

6. To make the orange spheres, take 200ml freshly squeezed orange juice, place in the rotary evaporator and rotate at 30°C for 1 hour at 50rpm, with the cooler set to -10°C to evaporate off 75% of the liquid. Take the remaining 50ml and add to 150ml duck stock. Mix this thoroughly with 1.2% sodium alginate and leave for several hours for the bubbles to escape (note – using a chamber vacuum machine can speed this process up).

7. Fill a dropping pipette with this thickened orange liquid, and slowly drip into a solution of 1% calcium chloride. This will allow spheres to form on contact with the calcium. Remove immediately and rinse before use.

8. Sweat off the shallot, vegetables, garlic, herbs and peppercorns in 10g butter until soft, add the Grand Marnier and reduce by half, add the orange juice and reduce by half and then add the duck jus. Bring to a simmer, skim and reduce to the correct consistency, season, restrain into a clean pan and keep hot.

9. Remove the duck breasts from the bags, drain, dry on kitchen towel and lightly season. Sear, to caramelise, in a non-stick pan in a little hot oil, drain and rest before carving.

10. Reheat the flaked leg meat in a little jus, enough to bind, season and form into small faggot shapes. Keep hot.

11. To dress on the plate for service, place the faggot in the centre, carve the breast and place beside. Arrange the orange spheres to garnish then sprinkle the duck crumb at the base of the plate and spoon a little sauce on the breast. Serve a sauceboat of sauce apart. This dish can be served with pommes fondants that are cooked in duck stock, haricot beans and glazed carrots or similar.

*When using liquid nitrogen, make sure you are not exposing any skin and special protection gloves and goggles need to be worn when handling liquid nitrogen.

Seared fillet of Black Angus Beef, Braised Shin Bon-Bon and Truffle Mash

Serves 4

Ingredients:

4 x 180g Centre cut Black Angus beef fillets

30g Butter

1 Clove of chopped garlic

1 tbsp Chopped fresh rosemary

1 tbsp Chopped fresh thyme

For the braised shin bon-bon:

200g Black Angus shin of beef

80g Mirepoix of vegetables

1 Sprig each of rosemary and thyme

½ tsp Tomato purée

500ml Chicken stock

500ml Veal stock

500ml Red wine

20ml Vegetable oil

Maldon sea salt and black pepper

1 Jacket potato, peeled and made into potato string

For the truffle mash:

600g Maris Piper potatoes

50ml Milk

50ml Double cream

250g Unsalted butter

1 Périgord truffle, cleaned and finely chopped

4ml White truffle oil

Maldon salt and ground white pepper

For the vegetables:

8 Baby carrots

4 Baby leeks

4 Baby turnips

250g Spinach, picked and washed

4 Bunches watercress, processed into a smooth purée

Method:

1. Heat the oil, add the mirepoix and sear with the rosemary and thyme until a golden brown colour has been achieved.

2. Add the tomato purée and cook out, add all the red wine and stocks and simmer.

3. Sear the shin of beef in a hot shallow pan and add to the simmering liquid to slowly braise for 4-5 hours.

4. When finished; reduce the stock to a gelatinous sauce, flake the shin meat and form into 4 balls, wrap in the prepared potato string and deep fry until golden brown. Keep in a warm place for service.

Method:

1. Bake the potatoes at 180°C until soft, and pass though a fine sieve into a clean bowl.

2. Add the milk, cream and half of the butter and beat in vigorously. Season with chopped truffle, the truffle oil and the salt and pepper. Retain warm for service.

Method:

1. Blanch the baby vegetables in boiling salted water and refresh quickly in iced water. When needed for service reheat in a little butter and seasoning and keep warm.

2. Wilt the spinach in a little butter and warm the watercress purée.

To serve:

1. Sear the steaks in the remaining butter (heat until foaming) with the teaspoons of rosemary and thyme. Baste the steaks gently, and when cooked leave to rest for a few minutes.

2. Slice the steaks in half and place onto a pool of the watercress purée, and on top of the wilted spinach, place the glazed vegetables around with the bon-bon and the truffle mash.

3. Finally, finish the sauce with a knob of butter and serve.

Pan-Roasted Fillet of Spiced Pork with a Herb Mousse, Sage Derby and Prune Bon-Bon, Wild Rice, Lentil and Spring Cabbage, Summer Vegetable Medley, Wild Mushroom Jus

Ingredients:

1 x 400g Pork fillet
Pinch mixed spice
20g Ground wild rice
10g Mixed fresh herbs

For the mousse:
1 Egg white
50ml Double cream
Trimmings from pork fillet
5g Mixed fresh herbs

For the vegetable garnish:
30g Extra fine french beans
8 Spears medium asparagus
100g Peas in pod
100g Spring cabbage
80g Chantenay carrots
40g Puy lentils
2 Shallots
1 Carrot
60g Wild rice
½ Red onion
500ml Vegetable stock
200ml Chardonnay

For the jelly terrine:
1 Cox's apple
1g Agar
1 Pink Lady apple
50ml Cider
50ml Organic apple juice
5g Chervil

For the bon-bons:
50g Sage Derby cheese
50g Fresh breadcrumbs
100g Californian prunes
2 Eggs
50g Ground wild rice
50g Flour

For the jus:
600ml Brown veal stock
200g Pork trimmings
100g Vegetable Mirepoix
50ml White wine
1 Herb bouquet garni
50g Mixed wild mushrooms

Method:

1. Wash and put the wild rice onto boil in vegetable stock. Reserve for service.

For the jus:
1. Fry and colour the pork trimmings, add the Mirepoix and the stock and bring to the boil, simmer and reduce. Pass through muslin and a fine chinois. Add the sautéed wild mushrooms, adjust seasoning and consistency.

For the pork:
1. Trim pork fillet and rub with ground wild rice and spices and herbs. Place the chilled pork trimmings into a blender and mince, add herbs, seasoning, egg whites and cream to create a mousseline. Spread on one side of the pork fillet, wrap in clingfilm and chill.
2. When ready to cook, poach the pork to set the mousse for 1 minute. Take off the clingfilm and pan-fry to colour, then place in an oven for 10 minutes. When cooked, remove from the oven and rest in a warm place until ready for service.

For the apple terrine:
1. Bring the cider, apple juice and agar to the boil then add the chopped apple and chervil. Leave to cool slightly. Place the mix in the lined terrine mould and allow to set in a refrigerator. At service point cut to shape and warm through.

For the bon-bon:
1. Mix grated Sage Derby cheese, breadcrumbs, egg and the chopped prunes.
2. Mould into 3 ball shape sizes, approximately 40g each. Pané using the flour and ground rice. Deep fry at service point.

For the prune purée:
1. Purée the prunes with a little stock and adjust the consistency and seasoning.
2. Wash and boil the puy lentils in vegetable stock and refresh. At service point, add to some sweated brunoise of celery, carrot, shallot and shredded spring cabbage.

For the vegetable garnish:
1. Place the baby carrots in water with sugar and salt with a little butter and begin to cook. Trim the asparagus spears and blanch in boiling salted water. Pod the peas and blanch in boiling salted water, refresh quickly in iced water. Trim the extra fine French beans and blanch in boiling salted water, refresh quickly in iced water.
2. At service point, réchauffe the vegetables and toss in butter and olive oil and seasoning.

Lamb Rack with Black Olive and Goat's Cheese, Slow Cooked Shoulder with Onions, Citrus Glaze and Pistachio, Tomato, Garlic, Thyme and Rosemary

Ingredients:

1 x 4 bone lamb rack, French trimmed to eye

1 Sprig and 1 leaf thyme and bay leaf

100g Pitted kalamata olives

150g Crumbly goat's cheese

For the shoulder:

500g Boned and trimmed lamb shoulder

100g Caramelised, sliced sweet onions

100g Unsalted butter

1 Sprig rosemary

1 Bay leaf

400ml Lamb stock (clarified)

1g Orange zest

0.5g Bergamot

0.5g Lemon zest

0.5% of clarified stock, gellan gum type F

50g Pistachio crumb

Maldon salt and ground black pepper

For the tomato and rosemary spheres:

500g Vine tomatoes

500ml De-ionised water

5g Calcium chloride

250ml Tomato concentrate

4g Sodium alginate

Maldon salt

250ml Rosemary water

Method:

Rack of lamb:

1. Season the lamb and then roll in clingfilm to shape, tie loosely.

2. Cover the bones with a clean kitchen cloth. Place into a vacuum machine on full power.

3. Cook in a water bath at 56°C for 25 minutes.

4. Blend the olives until fine. Dehydrate for 24 hours.

5. Crumble the goat's cheese into small pieces and also dehydrate for 24 hours.

6. Crush the cheese and olives in a pestle and mortar until very fine. Pass through a conical strainer.

Science tip: when using the dehydrator to dry fruits and vegetables, ensure that your samples are sliced very thinly. If they are too thick, the water evaporation at the surface may form a crust which will prevent water evaporation from the inside.

Lamb shoulder:

1. Season the lamb shoulder and seal in a hot pan. Chill quickly.

2. Place into a vacuum bag with the aromatic herbs and spices.

3. Cook in a water bath at 76°C for 16 hours.

4. Remove from the bag and mix with the onions, season well and roll into cylinders. Refrigerate until set.

5. Place the citrus zests into the lamb stock and place into the sonic homogeniser for 60 seconds to infuse the zest flavour into the stock.

6. Pass the stock through a chinois and place into the centrifuge set at 4000rpm for 30 minutes.

7. Pour off the clarified liquid, add 0.5% gellan gum type F and heat to activate it. Leave to cool slightly. Cut the shoulder into desired lengths.

8. Hold the piece of shoulder with a cocktail stick and dip into the stock.

9. Let the stock gel then dip again. Repeat until a layer of gel has formed. Place into the refrigerator. Once set, roll the shoulder carefully in the pistachio crumb.

Tomato and rosemary spheres:

1. Place the calcium chloride into the de-ionised water and whisk until dissolved.

2. Blend the tomatoes to a pulp in a blender and pass through muslin.

3. Place the liquid in the rotary evaporator and spin on a low heat setting to evaporate some of the water.

4. Add 2g of sodium alginate into 250ml of the concentrated tomato water and mix thoroughly with a hand blender.

5. Using a syringe drop the thickened tomato water into the chloride bath, leave to set then remove and wash in clean water.

6. Place the chopped rosemary into the water and place into the sonic homogeniser for 60 seconds. Pass off the rosemary and proceed as for the tomato spheres.

For the garlic purée:
10 Roasted garlic cloves

Garlic purée:
1. Pass the garlic through a drum sieve and emulsify with pine nut oil.

For the pine nut oil:
200g Pine nuts
50ml Stock syrup

Pine nut oil:
1. Roast the pine nuts until golden, mix with the stock syrup and blitz in a Thermomix until smooth.
2. Place into centrifuge bottles and place into the centrifuge set at 4000rpm for 30 minutes.
3. Pour off resulting oil and retain for service.

Thyme glass:
100g Isomalt
1 tbsp Thyme leaves

Thyme glass:
1. Cook the isomalt until lightly caramelised, leave to cool slightly, add the thyme and pour onto a silicone mat.
2. Once cooled and hardened, blend in a Thermomix until it has been ground to a powder.
3. Sprinkle a thin layer of powder onto a silicone mat and place into a 150°C oven.
4. Once melted remove and leave to cool until hardened.

Potatoes:
4 Maris Piper potatoes
500ml Clarified butter
1 Sprig thyme
1 Ripped bay leaf
2 Crushed garlic cloves

Potatoes:
1. Place the herbs and garlic into clarified butter heat to 80°C and remove from the heat, leave to cool for 30 minutes.
2. Slice the potatoes 3mm thick and cut out with a 1 inch cutter.
3. Place the potatoes into a vacuum bag with the butter.
4. Place the bag in a refrigerator, flat, but so the butter does not leak.
5. Once the butter has set, seal and cook in a water bath at 89°C for about 20 minutes.
6. Remove the potatoes from the bag and stack 1½ inches high, place a cocktail stick in the centre to hold them in place and place inside a dariole mould.
7. Half cover with butter and place into an oil bain-marie.
8. Cover and cook in a hot oven until crispy and golden.

Lamb rack with black olive and goats cheese, slow
cooked shoulder with onions, citrus glaze and
pistachio, tomato, garlic, thyme and rosemary

Desserts

Crêpes Suzette

This dessert was first served by Auguste Escoffier at the Savoy Hotel, London in the honour of French actress Suzanne Reichenberg (1853–1924) who worked professionally under the name Suzette. In 1897, Reichenberg appeared in the Comédie Française in the role of a maid, during which she served crêpes on stage.

Ingredients (serves 2):

4 Crêpes
½ litre Freshly squeezed orange juice
1 Lemon (juice only)
1 Large orange
8 Sugar cubes
1 measure Cognac
1 measure Grand Marnier
25g Unsalted butter

Method:

1. Grate 8 sugar cubes against a grated orange to obtain the orange zest flavour and colour on each side of the sugar cubes.
2. Place the sugar cubes in a pan at the restaurant guest's table that has been preheated.
3. Add the juice of half a lemon onto the sugar cubes.
4. Cook the sugar cubes to melt and eventually caramelise.
5. When the sugar is caramelised, add the orange juice. Let the juice reduce and then add the Grand Marnier.
6. Let the juice reduce a little more until the consistency of the liquid resembles a sauce.
7. Add the crêpes, one by one. Turn each crêpe in the sauce until they are completely covered.
8. Remove from the heat and fold each crêpe in a triangle shape.
9. Tilt the pan slightly towards the open flame on the stove and pour in the Cognac to immediately flambé the crêpes.
10. Sprinkle the flames in the pan with a little additional sugar.
11. Finish the sauce with a little butter to give it a shine.
12. Cover the crêpes once more with the sauce.
13. Serve 2 crêpes per person onto warm plates.
14. Serve to your guests immediately.

Opéra Cake with Blood Orange Sorbet

Ingredients:

For the almond sponge:

75g Icing sugar

2½ tbsp Soft flour

75g Ground almonds

3 Eggs

15g Unsalted butter, melted and cooled

3 Egg whites

1 tbsp Caster sugar

For the ganache:

200g 70% Cacao Barry Fleur de Cao chocolate, finely chopped

120ml Milk

110ml Double cream

50g Unsalted butter, softened

For the coffee syrup:

1½ tbsp Sugar

1½ tbsp Instant coffee

90ml Water

For the butter cream:

70g Caster sugar

1 Egg white

1 tbsp Instant coffee

100g Unsalted butter, softened

Method:

1. To prepare the sponge layer; preheat the oven to 220°C. Line a 20 x 30cm baking pan with parchment paper. In a large bowl, sift together the flour and icing sugar, then add the ground almonds. Mix well. Add the eggs, one at a time, and beat until pale. Add the melted butter.

2. Beat the egg whites until stiff, then gradually add sugar and continue beating until stiff peaks are obtained.

3. Add half of the beaten egg whites to the almond mixture, mixing well, and then incorporate the remainder, folding until just combined.

4. Pour onto the baking tray and spread evenly. Bake for 6-8 minutes, or until golden and springy when touched. Loosen the edges with a knife and carefully turn out onto a wire rack covered with a sheet of parchment paper. Allow to cool.

5. Place finely chopped chocolate in a heatproof bowl and set aside. Bring the milk and 30ml of the cream to a boil. Pour the hot liquid onto the chocolate. Wait 30 seconds, and then add the butter and mix until smooth. Let cool until a spreadable consistency is obtained.

6. To prepare the coffee syrup, place the sugar and 90ml of water in a pan and stir until dissolved. Bring to a boil and add the coffee.

7. To prepare the butter cream, place the sugar and 3 teaspoons of water in a heavy skillet and make a sugar syrup. Stir until the sugar is completely dissolved and then boil, without stirring, until syrup reaches soft-ball stage, between 116 and 118°C.

8. Beat the egg white until soft peaks are obtained. Continue beating while incorporating the hot syrup. Beat until mixture is cold. Dissolve instant coffee in 1tsp of boiling water, cool and add to butter. Add one half of the egg-white mixture and beat well, then gently fold in the remainder until well combined.

9. Using a sharp knife, divide the sponge into 3 equal sections and carefully peel off the parchment paper. Each should be 10 x 20cm (4 x 8 inches).

10. Soak the first section with a third of the coffee syrup, and then spread over half of the butter cream. Place the next section of sponge on top, then soak with coffee syrup and spread with half of the ganache. Place the last section on top, soak with remaining syrup and spread with the rest of the butter cream, taking care to smooth the surface.

11. Melt the rest of the ganache over a pan of very hot water. Bring the remaining cream to the boiling point and incorporate into ganache. Allow to cool until a smooth, spreadable consistency is obtained and spread over top of cake.

For the blood orange sorbet:

275ml Water

175g Caster sugar

6 Blood oranges, juice only (or 425ml of juice)

1 Lemon, juice only

Method:

1. For the sorbet, bring the water and sugar to the boil in a saucepan. Once the sugar has dissolved, simmer for 5 minutes to produce a stock syrup.

2. Remove from the heat and allow to cool, and then add the orange and lemon juice. Chill the mixture then churn in an ice cream machine and place in the freezer.

To serve:

1. Remove the sorbet from the freezer about 20 minutes before serving to allow it to soften.

2. Cut the Opéra into suitable portions and serve with the blood orange sorbet, some orange compote and a fine strip of praline on top.

Panna Cotta with Strawberry Compote

6 portions

Ingredients:

3 Gelatine leaves

250ml Milk

250ml Double cream

1 Vanilla pod split lengthways, seeds scraped out

25g Sugar

Method:

1. For the panna cotta, soak the gelatine leaves in a little cold water until soft.
2. Place the milk, cream, vanilla pod with the seeds and sugar into a saucepan and bring to a simmer. Remove the vanilla pod.
3. Squeeze the water out of the gelatine leaves, then add to the pan and take off the heat. Stir until the gelatine has dissolved.
4. Divide the mixture among 4 plastic tube moulds and leave to cool. Place into the refrigerator for at least an hour, until fully set.

For the strawberry tuiles:

255g Soft flour

255g Icing sugar

170ml Egg white

170g Butter

Dried strawberry pieces

Method:

1. Mix together all the ingredients and chill for 1 hour.
2. Spread mix on a template, sprinkle on strawberry pieces and bake for 8-10 minutes.
3. Leave to cool and dust with icing sugar.

For the strawberry compote:

400g Strawberries

250ml Stock syrup

2tsp Lemon juice

Method:

1. Boil the stock syrup.
2. Add the washed and prepared strawberries, simmer for 30 seconds.
3. Add the lemon juice and cool. Reserve for service.

To serve:

1. Carefully turn each panna cotta out onto a serving plate. Garnish and decorate as required with the tuile and strawberry compote.
2. Additional decorative elements can be used such as a strawberry gel, petit strawberry meringues and strawberry coulis.

Pink Champagne Jelly

Ingredients:

220g Caster sugar

190ml Water

6 Leaves gelatine

280ml Pink champagne

Method:

1. Soak the gelatine in cold water to soften.

2. Bring the sugar and water to the boil.

3. Remove from the heat and add the gelatine. Mix in to ensure that the gelatine has completely melted.

4. Cool and add the champagne making sure you have 578ml of jelly. Top up with more champagne if required.

For pink grapefruit sorbet:

200ml Water

175g Caster sugar

475ml Pink grapefruit juice

50g Glucose

Method:

1. Bring the water, sugar and glucose to the boil. Reduce the heat and simmer for 5 minutes.

2. Remove from the heat and cool down.

3. Add the pink grapefruit juice with some of the chopped flesh for added texture.

4. Chill the preparation in a refrigerator before churning in a sorbetière.

For rose cream:

200g Double cream

150ml Rose water

50g Caster sugar

Method:

1. Place the rose water and sugar into a pan onto a medium heat.

2. Bring to the boil and reduce for approximately 1 minute. Remove from heat and chill in a refrigerator.

3. Lightly aerate the double cream and add the rose syrup. Continue to whisk until the cream becomes firm and holds itself in peaks.

4. Store in a refrigerator until it is required for service.

Raspberry Soufflé, San Domingue Sorbet

Serves 8

Ingredients:

You will need 8 x No 1 sized ramekins

500ml Raspberry purée

110g Caster sugar (1)

55g Cornflour

500ml Egg whites

65g Caster sugar (2)

Method:

1. Place the raspberry purée and the 110g caster sugar (1) into a saucepan and heat slowly over a medium heat.
2. Dissolve the cornflour in enough water to make a smooth paste.
3. Add the dissolved cornflour and beat well. Maintain the raspberry purée on the heat to cook out and thicken the purée to a soft paste.
4. Remove from the heat and leave the raspberry preparation to cool.
5. Carefully grease the ramekins with softened butter, and place in a refrigerator to set. Repeat this process once more and then lightly coat the inside of the ramekins with caster sugar. Shake out any excess sugar.
6. Aerate the egg whites to soft peaks, whilst gradually adding the 65g caster sugar (2).
7. Fold half of the meringue mixture carefully into the raspberry preparation using a whisk until both mixtures have been completely combined, then carefully fold in the remaining whites.
8. Fill the ramekins to the very top and lightly tap in the dishes in your hand to ensure each dish is adequately filled.
9. Level off the top with a palette knife and clean the edges by running your thumb around the rim of each ramekin.
10. Wipe clean any droplets from the ramekins.
11. These can be stored in a refrigerator for between 3-4 hours before serving.
12. To serve, bake in the oven at 190-200˚C for 12-14 minutes.
13. Dust the tops with icing sugar and serve immediately with the sorbet, compote and tuile.

For the San Domingue chocolate sorbet:

250ml Milk

250ml Water

141g Caster sugar

55g Glucose

390g 70% Cacao Barry San Domingue dark chocolate

Method:

1. Bring the water, sugar and glucose to the boil and immediately leave to cool.
2. Separately, bring the milk to the boil, cool and add the chocolate to melt into the milk. Stir constantly.
3. Add the chocolate milk to the syrup preparation.
4. Mix together, strain through a fine chinois and freeze in a sorbetière. When the sorbet has formed, place into a container and leave in the freezer prior to service.

For the raspberry tuiles:

255g Soft flour

255g Icing sugar

170ml Egg white

170g Butter

Dried raspberry pieces

Method:

1. Mix together all the ingredients and chill for 1 hour in a refrigerator.
2. Spread the preparation onto a template, sprinkle on the dried raspberry pieces and bake for 8-10 minutes in a hot oven.
3. Remove from the oven and whilst still hot, bend the tuile to the required shape.

For the raspberry compote:

400g Fresh raspberries

250ml Stock syrup

2 tsp Lemon juice

Method:

1. Boil stock syrup and add the raspberries. Simmer for 30 seconds.
2. Add the lemon juice and cool down for service.

The classic 'Peach Melba'

The original Peach Melba recipe, as translated from Escoffier's words and sometimes served in our Escoffier Restaurant.

History

Peach Melba is a famous dessert, long a classic in Europe and much enjoyed in many other parts of the world. This mix of peaches and raspberries in a sauce over vanilla ice cream was created in the early 1890s by Auguste Escoffier, when he worked at London's Savoy Hotel. The name comes from Dame Nellie Melba, who at the time was one of the most celebrated opera singers. Through the dessert, Escoffier sought a way for Dame Melba to eat ice cream, something she loved but feared she couldn't eat because it would damage her singing voice.

The original name for Peach Melba was pêche au cygne or "peach with a swan." It referenced Dame Melba's performance in the Wagner opera Lohengrin to which Melba had invited Escoffier. The opera was part of the Knight of the Swan tradition and based on medieval tales where a knight arrives in a swan boat. Escoffier loved the swan boat used in the opera, and prepared the first pêche au cygne with a swan ice sculpture.

Later, as some accounts go, Escoffier re-managed the dessert when he went to work at the Ritz Carlton Hotel, and added raspberries to the peaches, renaming the dessert to Peach Melba so no one would forget its inspiration. It is this recipe that has become most famous and was most published in later cookbooks. This improved version as Escoffier made it is actually simple to make.

Most Peach Melba recipes call for you to blanch the peaches and remove their skins. If the peaches are very ripe, the blanching step may be unnecessary and skin removal on ripe peaches is easy. The peeled and sliced peaches are sprinkled with granulated sugar and allowed to macerate and chill. Raspberries in Escoffier's recipe were crushed and then strained, but this step is now made much simpler by using either a food processor or blender to turn the raspberries into a fine sauce. The sauce will be a little runny and should be thickened with powdered sugar. Escoffier recommended straining the crushed berries to remove seeds, and you can do the same if you don't care for seeds and want a smoother sauce.

When the peaches and raspberries are chilled, ice cream is placed in a dish, bowl or cup, and the peaches are layered on top. Next, raspberry sauce is poured over the peaches and ice cream to produce a wonderful sundae like confection that bursts with fresh taste. You don't, however, need to wait until these fruits are in season if you can get them frozen. You can certainly use frozen peaches and frozen raspberries, or even mixed berries to make a passable Peach Melba at any time of the year, though some people do claim that the best renderings of Peach Melba always use fresh fruit.

Ingredients:

6 Ripe, tender peaches
Sugar
1½ pints Vanilla ice cream
1 Heaping cup fresh ripe raspberries
1 Heaping cup powdered Sugar
6 tbsp blanched raw almond slivers
(optional)

Method:

1. Boil a medium pot of water. Keep a large bowl of ice water close by. Gently place a peach into the boiling water. Let the peach simmer for 15-20 seconds, making sure all surfaces of the peach are submerged. Remove from the boiling water with a slotted spoon and immediately plunge it into the ice water for a few seconds to cool.

2. Take the peach out of the ice water and place it on a plate. Repeat the process for the remaining peaches.

3. When all of the peaches have been submerged, peel them. Their skin should come off easily if they are ripe, thanks to the short boiling process. Discard the skins. Halve the peeled peaches and discard the pits.

> *Optional Step:* Place the peeled peaches in a large bowl of cold water mixed with 1tbsp fresh lemon juice or ascorbic acid powder. Let the peach halves soak for 10 minutes. Drain off the water and gently pat the peach halves dry with a paper towel.
> This step will help to keep the peaches from oxidizing and turning brown. Sprinkle the peach halves with sugar on all exposed surfaces. Place them on a plate in a single layer, and then place them in the refrigerator for 1 hour to chill.

4. Meanwhile, make the raspberry purée. Place the raspberries into a blender and pulse for a few seconds to create a purée. Strain purée into a bowl through a fine-mesh sieve, pressing down on the solid ingredients and agitating the mixture with a metal spoon to extract as much syrupy juice as possible. It will take a few minutes to extract all of the juice from the solids. When finished, you should only have seeds and a bit of pulp left in the strainer. Dispose of the solids.

5. Sift the powdered sugar into the raspberry purée, adding a little powdered sugar at a time, and whisking in stages till the sugar is fully incorporated into the syrup. It will take several minutes of vigorous whisking to fully integrate the powdered sugar into the syrup. Refrigerate the raspberry syrup for 1 hour, or until chilled.

6. Assemble 6 serving dishes. Scoop ½ cup of vanilla ice cream into each serving dish. Place 2 of the sugared peach halves on top of each serving of ice cream. Divide the raspberry sauce between the 6 dishes, drizzling the sauce over the top of the peaches and ice cream. Top each serving with a tablespoon of raw almond slivers, if desired. Serve immediately.

The classic 'Peach Melba'

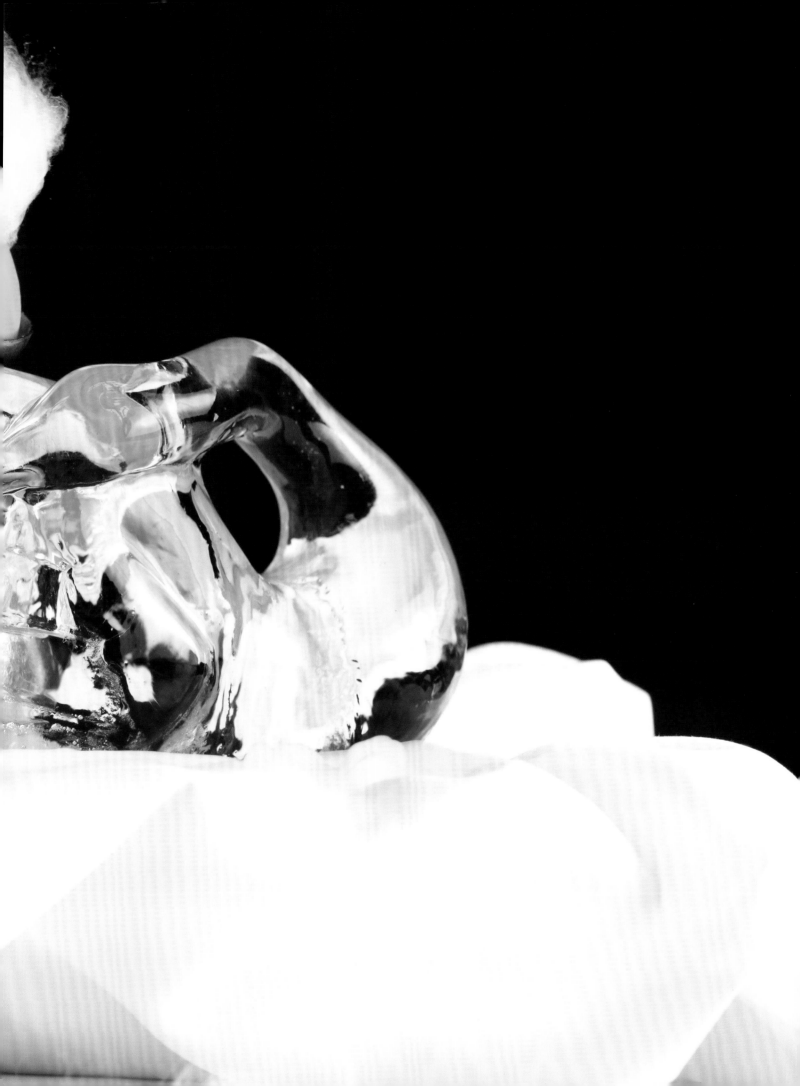

Chocolates

Blood Orange Caramel and Tonka Bean Chocolates

1 chocolate mould yields 24 pieces

Ingredients:

For the blood orange caramel:

120g Caster sugar
50g Cream
45g Glucose
60g Blood orange purée
20g Mango purée
110g Cacao Barry Papouasie milk chocolate

For the tonka bean ganache:

100g Cream
60g Vanilla yoghurt
10g Trimoline
4g Tonka beans
75g Cacao Barry Venezuela dark chocolate
175g Cacao Barry Papouasie milk chocolate

Preparing the chocolate moulds:

1. Gently fleck a chocolate mould with tempered red and the orange cocoa butter and then spray with tempered yellow cocoa butter.
2. Line with tempered milk chocolate (Cacao Barry Lactée Supérieure).
3. When set, pipe in equal quantities of the blood orange caramel and Tonka bean ganache.

Method:

1. Create a dry caramel with the caster sugar.
2. Warm the cream and glucose together and carefully add to the caramel.
3. Now add 2 two fruit purées and pour over the chocolate. Mix well using a hand blender.
4. Use this filling when the temperature has reached 35°C and pipe to half fill each chocolate mould. Leave to crystallise and set.

Method:

1. Warm the cream in a saucepan.
2. Infuse the Tonka beans in the cream for 20 minutes.
3. Strain the Tonka beans from the cream and add the vanilla yoghurt.
4. Add the pre-warmed chocolate and mix well with a hand blender.
5. Pipe into the moulds set with the blood orange caramel to just below the surface line of the chocolate mould.

Finishing:

1. Cap off with tempered milk couverture (Cacao Barry Lactée Supérieure) when the Tonka Bean ganache has crystallised and set. Turn out of the chocolate mould when set after 60 minutes and finish with a small chocolate pressed flower on top.

Coffee and Hazelnut – Hand-Piped Chocolates
Yields 24 pieces

Ingredients:

For coffee ganache:
160g UHT double cream
2g Coffee – good quality instant
20g Trimoline
110g Dark couverture 65% buttons
(Cacao Barry Madirofolo Madagascar
Millesime 2012)
50g Milk couverture 38% buttons
(Cacao Barry Lactée Supérieure)
20g Unsalted butter
10g Tia Maria

For the praline:
42g Icing sugar
60g Hazelnut powder – lightly roasted
20g Hazelnut paste
35g Milk chocolate (Cacao Barry
Lactée Supérieure), melted to 45°C
18g Chopped hazelnuts – lightly roasted

Method:
1. Bring to the boil the cream, coffee and trimoline.
2. Pour onto the combined dark and milk couvertures and blend to a smooth paste with a stick blender.
3. Add the unsalted butter and the Tia Maria.
4. Finish the emulsification of the ganache with a stick blender.
5. Leave to set and then pipe bulbs onto small praline discs (see below).

Method:
1. Mix together the icing sugar and hazelnut powder in a blender.
2. Add the hazelnut paste and the milk chocolate.
3. Quickly incorporate the chopped hazelnuts to retain a coarse texture.
4. Empty onto guitar sheet and cover with another sheet – roll to 3mm thick.
5. Freeze the sheet until firm enough to cut small discs on which to pipe bulbs of coffee ganache.

Finishing:
1. When the ganache is crystallised and set, dip into tempered dark chocolate (Cacao Barry Extra Bitter Guayaquil)
2. Place onto a bronze patterned transfer sheet if a decorative surprise underneath is fancied!
3. Decorate with a dusting of bronze powder tint, a tiny chocolate motif and a small toasted hazelnut on top.

Madagascan Vanilla Pralines

3 chocolate moulds yield 72 pieces

Ingredients:

690g Whipping cream

100g Milk

5g Madagascan vanilla pods

4g Madagascan vanilla natural extract

400g Cacao Barry Dark Tanzanie chocolate

50g Unsalted butter

Preparing the chocolate moulds:

1. Gently rub, with the tip of a finger into a chocolate mould, some tempered dark chocolate couverture.
2. Line with tempered milk chocolate (Cacao Barry Lactée Supérieure).
3. When set pipe in the following preparations (see ingredients).

Method:

1. Warm the cream, milk and vanilla together to blend and then bring to the boil. Leave to infuse for 30 minutes.
2. Pour this preparation onto the dark chocolate and blend well together.
3. When the ganache reaches a temperature of 35°C, blend in the unsalted butter.
4. Mix well using a hand blender.
5. Pipe into the moulds to just below the surface line of the chocolate mould.

Finishing:

1. Cap off with tempered milk couverture (Cacao Barry Lactée Supérieure) when the ganache has crystallised and set. Turn out of the chocolate mould when set after 60 minutes.

Strawberries and Cream Chocolates

1 chocolate mould yields 24 pieces

Preparing the chocolate moulds:

1. Gently fleck a chocolate mould with tempered white cocoa butter and then spray with tempered red cocoa butter.
2. Line with tempered milk chocolate (Cacao Barry Lactée Supérieure) or dark chocolate (Cacao Barry Fleur de Cao) if preferred.
3. When set, pipe in equal quantities of the jelly and ganache.

Ingredients:

For the Strawberry jelly:

240g Strawberry purée

48g Glucose

40g Caster sugar

2.25g Pectin

10g Lemon juice

Method:

1. Heat together the strawberry purée and the liquid glucose.
2. Sieve together the caster sugar and the pectin powder. Add this sugar and pectin mix to the heated strawberry purée and cook for 4 minutes, stirring with a whisk.
3. Finally, whisk in the lemon juice and remove from the heat to cool.
4. When the strawberry jelly mixture has sufficiently cooled, pipe into the chocolate moulds up to the halfway mark.

For the mascarpone ganache:

80g UHT double cream

40g Glucose

30g Trimoline

1 Vanilla pod

110g Mascarpone

340g White chocolate callets (Cacao Barry Zephyr)

5g Kirsch

Method:

1. Heat together the cream, glucose, trimoline and split vanilla pod.
2. Add the mascarpone and blend together.
3. Pour this over the white chocolate and add the kirsch.
4. Complete the emulsification of this ganache with a stick blender.
5. Pipe on top of the strawberry jelly to just below the surface line of the chocolate mould.

Finishing:

1. Cap off with tempered milk couverture (Cacao Barry Lactée Supérieure) when the mascarpone ganache has crystallised and set. No other decoration is required as the mould has already been sprayed with colours.

Petit Fours

Macaroons

Macaroons

Ingredients:

270g Egg whites

600g Icing sugar

12g Clear alcohol

5g Powdered colour – mixed into the alcohol removing all lumps

300g Sieved ground almonds

Flavouring (if required)

Method:

1. Aerate the egg whites over a bain-marie and work up to a temperature of 60°C.

2. Remove from the heat and continue whisking to cool the egg whites and thicken them slightly.

3. Incorporate the colour mixed into the alcohol.

4. Gradually add the sieved almonds and mix in until the preparation begins to drop in volume.

5. Add the flavouring and deposit into a piping bag with a plain tube fitted.

6. Pipe the macaroon mix onto siliconee lined baking sheets and then tap the sheet twice to settle the piped mixture.

7. Dust with a little coloured granulated sugar on each piped macaroon. Leave to skin for 20-30 minutes.

8. Bake in a preheated oven at 150°C on double baking sheets for approximately 10 minutes.

9. Turn the baking sheet around after 10 minutes and bake for a further 3-6 minutes.

10. Leave to cool slightly before removing from the siliconee and select an appropriate filling to pipe between two macaroon halves.

Pate de Fruits

Makes a 30cm x 20cm frame

For this recipe you can choose from many different types of fruit such as raspberry, cherry, mango and apricot. We always have a version of these as part of our petit four selection at the end of lunch or dinner.

Ingredients:

750g Fruit purée

150g Caster sugar (1)

20g Pectin

600g Caster sugar (2)

180g Glucose

Method:

1. Warm the fruit purée in a heavy based saucepan.

2. Whisk in the sugar (1) mixed in with the pectin.

3. Bring this to the boil and add the second quantity of sugar (2) and the glucose.

4. Cook to 105°C, and then add 8g acid solution (equal quantity citric acid and water).

5. Pour quickly into frame lined with silicone paper or clingfilm and leave to set.

6. Cut into rectangles or squares and roll in caster sugar.

Strawberry Delice

Ingredients:

For the strawberry mousse:
2 Egg yolks
62g Caster sugar
2 Leaves of gelatine
250ml Whipping cream
200g Strawberry purée

Method:
1. Whisk the egg yolks with the caster sugar over a bain-marie to create a sabayon.
2. Soak the gelatine in cold water to soften. Squeeze off the excess water and place into a pan with 50g of the strawberry purée.
3. Warm gently to dissolve the gelatine. Mix with the remainder of the purée.
4. Aerate the whipping cream to a soft ribbon stage.
5. Add the purée to the sabayon, and fold in the whipped cream.
6. Now pour into a suitable mould and set in a refrigerator.

For the shortbread base:
250g Soft flour
150g Salted butter
75g Caster sugar
¼ Vanilla pod, split with the seeds scraped out
Pinch of salt

Method:
1. Place the flour, softened butter, caster sugar, vanilla and salt into a bowl and mix until a smooth paste is achieved.
2. Place into some baking parchment and rest in a refrigerator for 30 minutes.
3. Pin out a thin sheet (5mm thick) of the paste and cut out suitable sized discs to complement the size of the delice moulds.
4. Bake in a preheated oven at 160°C until light and golden in colour.
5. When completely baked, sprinkle lightly with some additional caster sugar and leave to cool on a wire rack.

Finishing:
1. Neatly place on top of the shortbread discs some very fine, thin slices of fresh strawberry.
2. Place on top the strawberry mousse and decorate with a small white chocolate motif, small freeze dried strawberry pieces and serve as a petit four.

Afternoon Tea

Dobos Torte (The Westminster Version)

Ingredients:

For the Dobos sponge (makes one large tray):

8 Egg yolks	
8 Egg whites	
225g Caster sugar	
225g Butter	
170g Soft flour	
Orange zest	

Method:

1. Cream the butter and 125g of the caster sugar.
2. Add the egg yolks and incorporate by beating with a wooden spoon or on a mixing machine.
3. Aerate the egg whites and remaining sugar to create a light meringue.
4. Alternately fold the meringue preparation and sieved flour into the butter preparation.
5. Spread thinly onto a baking tray lined with siliconee paper and bake in a preheated oven set at 180°C for 12-15 minutes.

For the caramel cream filling:

250g Caster sugar	
50g Butter	
100ml Double cream	

Method:

1. Add a small amount of water to the caster sugar in a saucepan and over a medium heat cook to an amber caramel.
2. Immediately remove from the heat and add the butter and cream to make a thick cream. Continue stirring until the cream is smooth. Cool in a refrigerator until required.

For the ganache covering:

120g 64% Cacao Barry chocolate 'Extra-bitter Guayaquil'	
100g Double cream	
20g Glucose	
20g Grand Marnier	

Method:

1. Heat the cream and glucose in a saucepan.
2. Pour onto the chopped chocolate and blend with a hand blender until a smooth consistency has been obtained. Add the Grand Marnier at the last moment.

To assemble:

1. Cut the Dobos sponge into strips, the length of the tray and 7cm wide. Six strips will be needed.
2. Sandwich the strips together with the caramel cream. Set in a refrigerator for a few minutes to firm up.
3. Place the Dobos cake onto a wire rack and pour over the ganache to glaze the whole cake.
4. Slice into portions and decorate with some piped ganache and a chocolate motif.

Peach Melba Tartlets

Ingredients:

For the sweet pastry:

200g Plain flour

100g Butter

50g Sugar

60g Egg

2g Lemon zest

Method:

1. Rub the butter into the flour and combine egg and sugar, add a pinch of zest and then add to the flour and combine to form a paste (do not over work). Wrap in baking parchment and rest for 30 minutes in a refrigerator.

2. Roll out the paste and line the tart cases, blind bake with baking beans at 175˚C for 20 minutes.

For the crème patissiere:

250g Milk

2 Egg yolks

1 Egg

75g Sugar

2g Vanilla

20g Flour

5g Cornflour

Method:

1. For the crème pâtissière, place the milk onto a medium heat to infuse with the vanilla and bring up the temperature slowly to 95˚C (do not boil). Whisk the egg and sugar until light and creamy. Add the flour and cornflour to obtain a thick but smooth paste.

2. Pour on the warm milk slowly, constantly stirring.

3. Return to the heat in a clean pan continually stirring, and the preparation will gradually thicken. Remove from the heat and cover with a cartouche allowing the crème to cool.

For the sugar cage:

500g Sugar

2g Glucose

250g Water

Method:

1. Heat the sugar to be used for the cage to 121˚C (with a slight amber colour achieved).

2. Over the back of a lightly oiled ladle, drizzle the sugar from a spoon to form a cage. Leave to set and cool before removing from the ladle.

For the coulis:

1kg Fresh raspberries

200g Sugar

100g Apple juice

Method:

1. Place half the fresh raspberries into a bowl, cover and place over a double boiler for 10 minutes.

2. Place the sugar into water (2:1) and quickly boil until a thick syrup is achieved, after this strain the liquid from the raspberries and keep (discard the pulp).

3. Place the liquid into the apple juice with the remainder of the raspberries and sugar syrup and blend together to obtain a smooth coulis.

For the mascarpone quenelle:

250g Mascarpone cheese

1 Vanilla pod

25g Icing sugar

1g Gelatine (1 sheet)

125g Double cream

Method:

1. Combine the mascarpone with the vanilla seeds and icing sugar.

2. Lightly aerate the cream, and add the liquid gelatine into the mascarpone and fold in the cream.

3. With 2 small demi-tasse spoons, quenelle the mix and place on a tray in a refrigerator to set and chill.

For the poached peach:

5 Peaches

1kg Sugar syrup

1 Cinnamon stick

Method:

1. Take the fresh peaches and poach them whole in sugar syrup with a stick of cinnamon.

2. Once cooked, allow to cool, and then cut the cheek flesh off to use.

For the finished piece:

125g Melted white chocolate

10 Tart cases

10 Mascarpone quenelles

10 Sugar cages

250ml Coulis

10 Poached peach cheeks

250g Crème patisserie

To finish:

1. Brush melted white chocolate on the inside of the tart case, fill with the crème pâtissière. Place a little coulis on crème patisserie.

2. Cut a "v" groove into top of peach. Place on the top of tart and pour coulis into groove. Top with a quenelle of mascarpone going across the coulis. Place sugar cage over the top.

179

Chocolate cake with praline cream and ganache glaze

Ingredients:

For fudge cake:

170g Butter

500g Caster sugar

170ml Olive oil

340ml Water

140g Cocoa powder

170ml Milk

3 Eggs

340g Soft flour

40g Baking powder

Method:

1. Place the water, butter and olive oil into a saucepan and bring to the boil.
2. Reduce the heat and add the cocoa powder, mix well until any lumps have dispersed.
3. Add the caster sugar and mix – remove from heat.
4. Leave the mixture to cool, and combine the eggs and milk together before gradually incorporating to the cocoa preparation.
5. Mix in the sieved flour and baking powder.
6. Place the mix into 20cm square baking tin, lined with baking parchment and bake in a preheated oven at 180°C for approximately 35 minutes.

For the praline cream:

100g Cacao Barry Praline (Favourites Hazelnut)

200g Double cream

Method:

1. Beat the praline for a few seconds to soften.
2. Whisk together the cream and praline until soft peaks have formed.
3. Reserve in a refrigerator until required.

For the ganache glaze:

150g Cacao Barry 55% Dark Couverture Excellence

120g Double cream

25g Glucose

Method:

1. Place the cream and glucose into a saucepan and bring to simmering point.
2. Cool slightly and carefully stir in the chocolate.
3. Finish briefly with a hand blender to create a smooth texture.

Finishing:

1. Cut 3 long strips from the chocolate cake, approximately 6cm wide.
2. Onto each strip, pipe a line of praline cream with a large plain piping tube and leave in a refrigerator or freezer to set.
3. Pour the ganache glaze over the prepared strips, sitting on a wire rack, and leave to set. You should only need to glaze the cake once. Leave to set in a refrigerator.
4. Cut into suitable portion sizes and serve.

Graduation

The certificates and awards have all been handed out. Speeches have been spoken. Applauding hands are clapped out and tired. Now it's time for the graduands to return to The Vincent Rooms as graduates; to toast their newfound alumni status.

The now-ex-pupils file out of St Stephen's Church, a sea of smiling faces and mortarboards. They turn left onto Rochester Row and – what's this? It's Westminster Kingsway College's current first- and second-year students, dressed in their chef whites and neckerchiefs, lining the street to congratulate their peers. They don't clap, though. Instead they applaud the achievements of the young chefs in a much more fitting way: by banging pots and pans.

It's the perfect way to conclude a graduation ceremony for the hospitality industry's stars of tomorrow. The graduates, who knew nothing about it, clearly agree, their

T he pots 'n' pans procession is a new tradition for the Westminster Kingsway College graduation, having been dreamt up by Gary Hunter on his way to the ceremony. "I got the idea from an East End New Year's Eve custom," he says. "Everyone goes out into the street with saucepans to 'bang in' the New Year." But in a place with as much history as this, some traditions date back much further.

The venue used for the ceremony, St Stephen's Church, shares its roots with the college itself. Both were made

As Westminster Kingsway College's head of culinary arts and hospitality, Gary acts as master of ceremonies at the graduation, delivering an introductory address and conducting proceedings throughout. Geoff Booth, assistant principal, also gives a speech, as do representatives from two organisations with strong and historical links to Westminster Kingsway College: Chris Basten, chairman of the Craft Guild of Chefs (the current incarnation of the group that founded the college) and Bev Puxley, Master of the Worshipful Company of Cooks, a former Westminster

Culinary Arts, Hospitality and Food & Beverage Service Graduation Award Prizes 2013

Sponsored by Churchill Commemorative Plate and Russums Voucher

Iwan Kriens Best All Round Chef Student for 2013:
Giorgio Finnochio

Emile Lefebvre Pastry Chef Diploma Student of the Year:
Stephen Smith

John Lindsay Best Restaurant Service Diploma Student of the Year:
Kristian Shields

César Ritz Best Hospitality Student of the Year:
Mirko Notturno

Sir Isidore Salmon Advanced Diploma Culinary Student of the Year:
Sarah Marshall

Auguste Escoffier Espirit de Corps Chefs Trophy:
Joseph O'Neill

The Michael Hollingsworth Cup for the Best Competition Chef:
Megan O'Mahoney

John Huber Espirit de Corps Pastry Chefs Trophy:
Edward Moseley

Restaurant Association of Great Britain Espirit de Corps Restaurant Service Trophy:
Sarah Collis

Louis Darsonval Cup Most Improved Chef Student:
William Procter

Most Improved Pastry Student:
Jeremy Ferdman

Most Improved Hospitality Student:
Viola Herber

Most Improved Restaurant Service Student:
Jasmine Robinson

Reunion Des Gastronomes Wolsten-Croft Trophy for Outstanding Achievement:
Stephen Smith

Index of recipes

Duck à L'Orange, duck skin 'crumb', orange 'spheres' and an orange and Grand Marnier jus

Acknowledgements

We would like to thank the following:

To the Culinary Arts and Hospitality Team at Westminster Kingsway College for their incredible passion, hard work and inspiration

To the Principal, Andy Wilson, and the College Executive Team for their unstinting support

To Geoff Booth, Assistant Principal, for his valuable direction and encouragement

To Hannah Skeggs and the Marketing Team for their guidance and collaboration

To the Board of Governors for their guardianship

To Jodi Hinds for her visionary and creative photography

To Adam Kay for his careful management and revealing words of visualization

To the Craft Guild of Chefs for their backing and sharing of historical text and images

To all our sponsors, friends, neighbours and supporters that help us achieve and realise our student's dreams for their careers

To the current student cohort for their motivation and dedication – you are the future stars of the industry

To all of our alumni and Old Students Association – you are the family that stimulates our history and encourages our work

To Renee Anderson and her excellent Library and Resources Team for the historical facts and photography

To the Royal Academy of Culinary Arts and the Master Chefs of Great Britain for the support of our curriculum and students

To the reader – we hope that you will be inspired to visit us soon

To our future students – we want you be our next Jamie Oliver or Sophie Wright